puppy
training
for kids

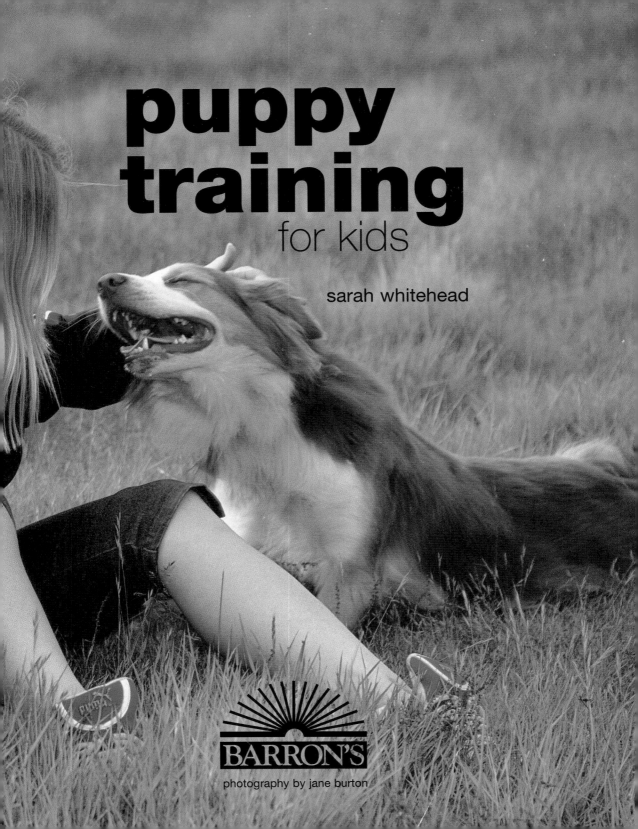

puppy
training
for kids

sarah whitehead

BARRON'S

photography by jane burton

First edition for the United States and Canada published in 2001 by Barron's Educational Series, Inc.

First published in 2001 under the title of *Puppy Training for Kids*
Text and design © Thalamus Publishing 2001

All inquiries should be addressed to:
Barron's Educational Series, Inc.
250 Wireless Boulevard
Hauppauge, NY 11788
http://www.barronseduc.com

Library of Congress Catalog Card Number:
00-112271
International Standard Book Number:
0-7641-1940-0

Project Editor: Warren Lapworth
Design: Roger Kean and Joanne Dovey
Illustrations: Oliver Frey
Four-Color Separation: Michael Parkinson

Printed and bound in Spain by Graficromo S.A.
9 8 7 6 5

Picture Acknowledgments

All photographs by Jane Burton and Kim Taylor/Warren Photographic, except 19 (bottom left) by Hazel Taylor. Additional computer work by Mark Taylor/Warren Photographic.

Models and puppies
Jumaane Bant with Joker
Marcia Blake with Henry
Siân Houghton with Bess
Louise Chambers with Sophie
Grace Cole-Hawkins with Fidget and Rolo
Jaye and Siân Gearing with Bebe
James and Daniel Mackenzie with Brak and Bobby
Emily Main with Misty and Wellington
Kathryn Main with Molly and Tansy
Natasha and Christopher McNaughton with Tommy and Gem
Ben Monks with Specs, Lollipop, and Blaze
Latasha Murphy with Bobby and Misty
Laurrie Murphy with Zena and Oliver
Ross Pankhurst with Inka
Peter Richards with Pipit
Bradley Ruddick with Tig
Jodie Ruddick with Fleck
Luke Stent with Jorge
Adelle and Gemma Tracey with Chip and Fly

a note for parents

This book has been written to encourage children of all ages to take an active part in caring for and training a new puppy.

Children are often exceptionally good at communicating with animals and can develop many different skills and learn the value of kindness and compassion through interacting with them.

All the exercises in this book are designed to be fun and friendly for both child and puppy, but they should always be supervised when they interact. It is therefore recommended that adult and child read the book together and that all training and care is done with adult supervision.

If you are concerned about your dog's behavior, especially toward children, contact your veterinarian for advice and a referral to a behavior or training specialist.

table of contents

introduction

There can be nothing more exciting than owning a puppy. Dogs are fun, friendly, and make great companions. They are happy to be active when you are full of energy, and to sit quietly when you just need a friend to be with.

Owning a puppy means taking responsibility for the health and happiness of another living being, not just for a day or a week, but for all the years that he or she will live with you. Your puppy will need to go for a walk — even if the weather is bad outside. Your puppy has to be fed and played with — even when you are busy with friends — and needs training to understand how to live with people. Caring for your puppy is fun, exciting, and very rewarding.

Don't delay, start your training now — your puppy won't be a puppy for long. Dogs grow much more quickly than humans! In the first six months of their lives, dogs can easily reach their adult height, and can run, jump, and behave like adults, while many human babies are still unable to walk, talk, or even crawl, as the chart on this page shows.

puppy 2–4 weeks
child 1–2 years

puppy 12–18 weeks
child 8–11 years

your puppy's development compared to a human's

(Based on a medium-sized mixed breed)

puppy 4–8 weeks
child 3–4 years

puppy 8–12 weeks
child 5–7 years

puppy 9–12 months
child 15–17 years

puppy 5–9 months
child 11–14 years

your dog's first year

two weeks to four weeks

Puppies are born blind and deaf. Just like a human baby, they rely on their mother for food, warmth, and comfort. At about two weeks of age, puppies start to open their eyes, and begin to hear noises. By three weeks they can walk, although they may still be a little wobbly! At this stage, puppies are eager to explore the world around them, but need to be close to their mom all the time, since they cannot keep themselves warm.

From the moment they are born, puppies have a very well developed sense of smell. Dogs have over 200 million scent-receiving cells in their noses! Puppies learn to recognize their mother's smell, so they can crawl toward her if they are parted from her.

filling out

All puppies are cute and cuddly in their first few weeks. Their coats may change in texture and color quite dramatically in this time, and their shape gradually becomes less rounded and more square as the weeks go by. Some breeds are almost unrecognizable as puppies — for example, Dalmatians are born pure white all over. It is only after a few days that their spots begin to show and darken.

four weeks to eight weeks

After four weeks, puppies can walk, run, and play with each other and with toys. They are very curious and want to explore as much as possible. At

top: *At one day old, the pup's most sensitive organ is the most obvious — the nose!*

left: *Puppies huddle together for warmth — and for security.*

this stage, puppies develop very small, sharp teeth. Just like toddlers, they put things in their mouths to see what they taste like and to find out how they react.

Children at the same stage (three to four years) can talk. Puppies too are learning a language — but they learn to speak to each other using body language. One puppy may walk over to another and wag its tail or lift up a paw. This means that he or she wants to play, and the brother or sister understands this move. A "play bow" is easily recognized — here the puppy dips its head and front legs to the floor, but leaves its bottom sticking in the air. This is a clear invitation to play.

At about four or five weeks of age, puppies start to eat solid food. This means that they become more independent, because they don't need to rely on their mother's milk. To begin with, they need to learn how to chew food properly. Sometimes, puppies get bored with their meal and may play with it instead of eating it.

At four weeks the eyesight is well developed.

play-bites

Puppies play with their jaws and their paws. Sometimes their play can become quite rough. If one puppy bites another too hard, the victim is likely to squeal, and all play will stop. This teaches the pups to be careful and not to hurt each other when playing.

eight weeks to twelve weeks

Most puppies go to their new homes at eight weeks old. It must be strange for a puppy to leave his mother and litter-mates (brothers and sisters) at this time — imagine leaving home when you are only five! Puppies of this age split their time in three ways: eating, playing, and sleeping.

In their first few days in a new home, most puppies spend time investigating and becoming familiar with their new family. It is important that the puppy has a place to sleep and is not disturbed when in his bed.

Puppies are very supple and flexible. This means that they sometimes fall over, go head over heels and are even able to lie out flat on the floor with their legs out behind them.

Puppies try to chew almost anything that they can reach with their mouths. Puppies don't understand the difference between a stick and a table leg — it's all chew toys to them! This means that you will need to provide suitable toys for your pet to play with. Hard rubber toys, chews, and rag toys are all ideal.

learning manners

All puppies need to learn to behave
respectfully toward older dogs and people.
Basic training and lots of play and contact with
dogs and people is necessary now.
Greeting you

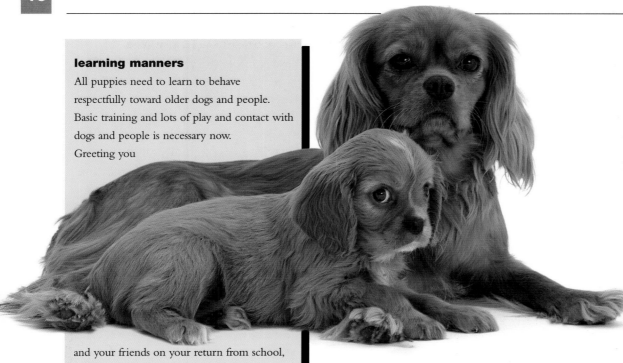

and your friends on your return from school,
learning to wait until it is safe to cross a street
and walking on a leash all need to be mastered.

*Between the ages of eight to 12 weeks, puppies
need to learn about the world.*

twelve to eighteen weeks

During this time, puppies are learning as
much as possible about the world. They
discover what is fun and what isn't. Puppies of
this age need to go to "school," just like
human children, to learn how to behave
when in the company of other dogs and
people. Many exercises, such as sitting when
told, and tricks of all kinds can be taught to
puppies of this age — they are so anxious to
learn and play.

At this stage your puppy is likely to behave
in a way that reflects his breed. Terriers, for
example, love to dig. Retrievers and other
gundogs nearly always love to carry objects
around in their mouths, while Collies and

other herding dogs may try to treat you like
sheep and round you up!

five months to nine months

This is the dog's teenage stage. Dogs of this
age often look rather gangly and "leggy," and
may be clumsy in their movements. They are
still learning about the world but are now
much more confident. Dogs of this age need
lots of training and firm rules in the home. It
may have been cute when your puppy slept
on the bed at only 12 weeks old, but now he
probably steals all the covers!

Going to training classes will help your
puppy understand human words and actions.
Your dog cannot speak or understand English,

so it is up to you to teach him the meaning of every word you use. Using rewards, such as food, toys, and praise in a light, happy voice, is very important, and the exercises should always be fun. This is because dogs, like humans, learn best when they are enjoying themselves.

Most "teenage" dogs enjoy physical activity, such as running, jumping, and balancing. Exercise is important to keep the body fit and the mind calm. Teaching your dog to chase a ball or toy and retrieve it is great fun and means you don't have to run as far as your dog.

puppy meets dogs

It is important that your puppy still meets and plays with other dogs. All dogs need to practice their communication skills with each other. This means there will be less risk of fights between them.

nine months to 12 months

Your dog is now an adult. Although your pet may become broader and more muscular, he is likely to have reached full height.

Some dogs never seem to behave as if they are grown up, while others are calm and sensible even at an early age. Although training can help to ensure that dogs behave well, some breeds are often excitable and clownish even as adults: Boxers and Dalmatians could be described this way.

wolf in dogs' clothing

All dogs need food, water, shelter, comfort, and companionship. They are social creatures, which means that they should live in family groups. Dogs are descended from wolves, and although they may not look much like wolves, many of the ways in which they behave are similar. For example, most dogs love to chase and catch toys. This is like a wolf hunting and chasing prey to eat.

Dogs are social creatures, and enjoy the company of their canine friends.

how your puppy works
1 smell and taste

smell

From the moment they are born, dogs have an amazing sense of smell. Even though newborns cannot see, hear, or walk, they can detect the scent and warmth of their mother and will crawl toward her to find food.

As time goes on, the puppy's sense of smell

A dog's nose is cool and moist to allow scent particles in the air to be captured.

improves. By the time she is adult, a dog's sense of smell far outstrips ours — it is thought that it is at least one million times better!

Puppies and dogs of all kinds use their sense of smell to communicate with each other.

This is why they like to sniff the ground and areas where other dogs might have been. Messages left by other dogs can be "read" by the dog's sense of smell, almost like humans read newspapers. Sniffing other dogs acts as an introduction. A dog's individual smell can give another dog information about her health, her sex, and even how friendly she might be.

Dogs also use their sense of smell to track down and hunt for prey. Their wild ancestors, wolves, needed to be very skilled at this to find food, and today dogs' hunting skills are used in sports such as tracking, and even to find and save people trapped in wreckage after earthquakes.

how the nose works

Just like us, the dog has a sensitive lining or membrane inside the nose. Tiny scent particles in the air are dissolved by the moisture on the dog's nose and inside the mouth, and then absorbed by the membrane. These scent messages are "read" by a special area in the brain to allow the dog to recognize smells.

Brain

Scent

Olfactory bulb

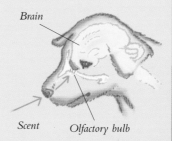

taste

It is not known exactly how much dogs can taste. Some dogs enjoy certain foods more than others, and it is likely that they can detect bitter, sweet, sour, and salty tastes, but perhaps not in the same way that we do.

Some dogs seem able and willing to eat anything and everything — and even enjoy unusual flavors, such as garlic or onions. Others are unwilling to try anything new and won't eat any food they have not tried before.

above: *Scent is vital to dogs — these puppies are sniffing the dewy grass where rabbits have been grazing.*

below: *Dogs sniff each other to give information about themselves. Here a Lakeland Terrier-Border Collie cross greets a black Lurcher nose-to-nose.*

taste aversion

Dogs sometimes make instant associations with the taste of specific foods. A dog that is sick after eating one type of food may avoid it afterward for a long time. This is called "taste aversion" and is a basic response to stop dogs eating foods that might be bad for them.

smelling people

Dogs can recognize people simply by the way they smell. Dogs have even been known to remember people that they have met only once before by recognizing the person's scent. However, even dogs may be confused by identical twins!

2 sight

When puppies are born, they cannot see at all. Their eyes are shut to begin with, so they are blind for about the first two weeks, until the eyes start to open. Once fully open, a puppy's eyesight is probably a little blurred, but this soon clears so that they can see their litter-mates, their mother, and the world around them.

Compared to human vision, dogs' eyes are more sensitive to light and movement, but they can't see the outline of objects so well.

above: *This Border Collie puppy is ten days old and cannot yet open his eyes. For the one-year-old Saluki Lurcher,* **below***, eyesight is almost as important as smell for hunting down prey.*

Your dog is able to spot even the tiniest insect in the grass, as long as it is moving, but will have trouble seeing it if it keeps perfectly still.

Different breeds of dog have a wider range of vision than others. This is because some breeds have been specially bred to be able to spot prey at a great distance. The Afghan Hound, for example, has his eyes set wide apart and to the side of his head, which allows him to see a wider area than the Bulldog, whose eyes point straight ahead.

Dogs can see better than humans at dusk or when the light is poor. However, they do not possess the same cells in the eye that relate to color vision that humans have, so they cannot see the range of colors we can.

catch!

Dogs are very good at judging distances. This means that if you throw a ball for your dog, he knows how far and how fast to run to be able to catch it. Some dogs are so good at this that they compete in Frisbee-catching.

At 14 days, the eyes are just beginning to open.

Dogs have a third eyelid. This is usually only seen if the dog is unwell.

Dogs produce tears, although not when they are unhappy, like humans do. A dog's tears are produced to keep the eyes clean and moist.

Unlike humans, dogs have a third eyelid that lies hidden in the corner of each eye. This is rarely seen, unless the animal is ill. The third eyelid protects the eye by moving across its surface.

"seeing" with other senses

Old dogs often lose part of their sight, and some become completely blind. Remarkably, many still enjoy life and can find their way around the home and yard by memorizing where furniture and objects are placed and using their senses of smell and touch.

how the eye works

The eye is a globe, filled with liquid. It is held in the eye socket in the skull by strong muscles. These muscles allow the eye to move up, down, and from side to side, which helps the dog to see movement out of the corners of its eyes.

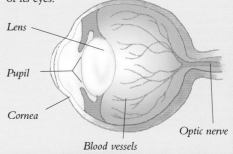

Lens

Pupil

Cornea

Optic nerve

Blood vessels

The Saluki Lurcher spots something moving in the bushes and goes into the characteristic pose called "pointing."

3 hearing

Most owners know that the quiet rustle of a sack of cookies is enough to bring their dog running! This is how sensitive your puppy's hearing is. Wolves and wild dogs need to have excellent hearing to help them find prey, defend the pack against intruders, and communicate with other dogs.

Tiny puppies have almost no sense of hearing. Within a few days of being born, pups are able to hear loud noises, and after only a few weeks can hear far better than we can. A young, healthy dog is able to detect a sound in six-hundredths of a second and, by using muscles in the outer ear to help guide sound into the inner ear, can hear noises four times further away than a human can.

Dogs can also shut off the inner ear to block out noise, so they can concentrate on a specific sound — which may explain why your puppy sometimes seems to ignore you when it wants to, especially if it is having fun!

left: *This puppy tilts her head to listen intently to unusual sounds.*

right: *Cavalier King Charles Spaniel Rosie cocks a lacy ear.*

deafness

Sadly, some puppies become deaf very early. This is more common in some breeds than others, particularly white ones. Dalmatians, Bull Terriers and white Boxers seem particularly prone to this problem and may be born deaf in one or both ears. Sometimes it is hard to tell that a puppy is deaf until she leaves the litter, although veterinarians are now able to test puppies' hearing at an early age.

Deaf dogs can still lead enjoyable and active lives. Lots of time and effort is needed to train deaf puppies, but it is possible and very rewarding. Deaf dogs can quickly learn to watch hand signals instead of following voice commands in training, and can make good pets, if treated with patience and given help.

Quick Tip — high sounds

The sensitivity of a dog's hearing can mean that some high-pitched sounds or very loud noises can affect her ears. Training should therefore be done calmly and quietly, with soft commands, rather than shouting.

head tilting

Dogs often tilt their heads when they are trying to locate a sound, or if they are puzzled by a certain noise. Puppies often look very cute when they do this — tipping their heads from side to side as if they are listening to every word you say. Look at the ones below!

how the ear works

The ear is made up of four parts: the ear flap, the external ear canal, the middle ear, and the inner ear. The size and shape of the ear flap varies between breeds and types of dog. The flap protects the inner ear by covering it, and also helps to funnel the sound through the ear canal to the ear drum.

Beyond the ear drum is the middle ear, which contains three small bones that transmit sound vibrations from the ear drum to the inner ear. Inside the inner ear, the cochlea converts these vibrations into signals that are sent to the brain.

The inner ear also controls the dog's sense of balance. These allow the dog to run, turn, and jump, landing on all four feet with ease.

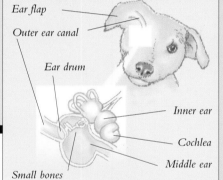

Ear flap
Outer ear canal
Ear drum
Inner ear
Cochlea
Middle ear
Small bones

left: *Some breeds, such as this nine-week-old Siberian Husky, have upright ears.*

right: *Up or down? This pup's ears are not yet fully developed.*

4 touch, warmth, and keeping cool

For the first two weeks of their lives, puppies rely almost totally on their sense of touch and their sense of smell. At this stage, they cannot keep themselves warm, and so must cuddle up to their mother and litter-mates to share body heat.

Once puppies have left the litter and live in a home with their new owners, they must become used to being touched differently. Most puppies love being stroked by their owners, but not many enjoy being hugged. The best places to touch your dog are normally the chest and belly. Many dogs like this so much that they roll over to have their tummies tickled.

Dogs can feel heat, cold, pain, and pleasure through their skin. Their noses are also very sensitive to touch and should never be smacked. It is thought that dogs' whiskers help them to locate objects by touch. The hair and nails are much

below: *These newly born puppies need to cuddle up to their mother and litter-mates to keep warm.*

above: *Many dogs love to have their chest tickled.*

like ours and can be trimmed without discomfort.

Feet, mouth, and tail are usually the most sensitive areas for a dog that does not like being handled. Touching your puppy all over its body and giving food or games as a reward is an important part of everyday care.

Dogs that live together or know each other well are likely to use touch as reassurance and may often sleep by resting close to each other or even in the same bed! This probably gives them the same feelings of safety and warmth that they had when they were puppies, snuggled up with their mother and litter-mates.

keeping warm

Many dogs have a remarkable ability to keep themselves warm, even in very cold weather. Some breeds have been specially bred to cope with snow and ice, and have thick hair with a second coat underneath that is virtually weatherproof. Breeds such as Siberian Huskies

even have hair covering their feet to keep them warm.

Some owners provide jackets or coats for their dogs to wear in winter, and this helps some smaller, thin-coated dogs to keep warm and keeps water from reaching the skin (see left).

They are available in lots of different styles and colors, from knitted, woolly jumpers to waterproof, waxed jackets.

chill out!

Keeping cool can be more difficult than staying warm for many dogs. This is because they cannot sweat like we do. Dogs can only lose heat through their feet and mouths, by panting. Dogs in enclosed spaces may find it very difficult to keep cool in the summer, and being shut in an automobile in hot weather is a real danger. In hot weather they need fresh air, shade in which to rest, and plenty of water to drink. Many dogs, like the Border Collie in the picture above, love to cool off by swimming in the sea or in freshwater pools.

hairstyles

Some breeds' coats are clipped into certain shapes or styles to keep the dogs cool or warm. The Standard Poodle was originally bred to retrieve ducks from water. Its coat was trimmed into a distinctive shape, with long hair left at the chest and at the knees, wrists, and ankles to keep it warm while swimming.

5 movement

Simply having four legs instead of two gives dogs greater balance and speed than humans. Nearly all dogs can outrun people, and certain breeds are really fast. Greyhounds, for example, can reach speeds of up to 43mph (70 km/h).

above: *The first tentative steps of this three-week-old toddler are a long way from the joyous galloping of his older cousins* **below**.

the dog's skeleton

The dog's skeleton supports and protects the body's internal organs. Bones are hollow tubes, filled in the middle with bone marrow. Blood vessels nourish this living structure, by entering the bone though tiny holes. This allows a broken bone to re-grow and mend itself.

Unlike us, dogs do not have a collar bone. Instead, the front limbs are held in place by muscles. This allows the dog flexibility to run, jump, swim, and turn.

Dogs are able to walk, trot, canter, and gallop, as well as jump, twist, swim, and even crawl. Large breeds often choose to lope along in a loose walk, while the smaller, more sprightly breeds may show a high-stepping trot.

Dogs will use up energy only when they have to, in work or play. This means that the wolf and most pet dogs will trot to cover long distances. Sled dogs, such as Siberian Huskies and Alaskan Malamutes, are the long-distance specialists. At a speed of up to 25 mph (40 km/h), they can travel 1,000 miles (1,600 km) in less than ten days.

how fast can they run?
Wolf: 35 mph (56 km/h)
Greyhound: 43 mph (70 km/h)
Cheetah: 70 mph (113 km/h)

why does my dog stretch?

Dogs often stretch when they first wake up, to warm up their muscles and because it feels good — just like stretching after waking in the morning feels to us. Many dogs stretch one end first and then the other, by pushing their front end to the floor and stretching their hind legs, then their neck and shoulders.

swimming

Dogs are usually good swimmers. Although it may take a few sessions for a dog to become confident in the water, most really enjoy it. Some breeds have been especially bred to swim. The Newfoundland, for example, was bred to pull fishing nets out of the water and to help rescue drowning people. He even has webbed feet that act like flippers in the water.

can dogs climb?

Dogs are not very good at climbing. Some individuals are said to be able to climb out of enclosures, but these feats are rare. Dogs that are trained to compete in working trials need to climb a six-foot vertical wall, called the scale, but most do this by scrambling up the face of the wall, rather than climbing.

Galloping is used when a burst of high speed is necessary. This pace uses a large amount of energy and so is only used for short distances. Breeds such as the Greyhound are the sprinters of the dog world and can reach fantastic speeds over short distances.

Flexibility is also important for many dogs. Some can turn in the air to catch a ball or even a bird, while others can squeeze themselves into narrow underground burrows and can even turn around while inside. Collies and other herders can drop to the ground then spring back into action at the slightest signal.

what your puppy needs

All puppies have basic needs. Just like us, they need food and water to survive and good care to ensure that they stay fit and healthy.

For the first few days, give your new dog the same type of food she ate in her former home, to make sure the new pet does not get a stomach upset.

Your puppy needs a bowl filled with fresh drinking water available at all times. It can be a task to make sure that this is always fresh and clean, but it is very important to a puppy's health.

Just like children, puppies need to be protected against diseases, and vaccinations can help to keep them healthy. Puppies are given vaccinations by having a series of injections, into the loose skin at the back of the neck. These are not painful, although they may startle the puppy a little.

Puppies also need to visit the veterinarian if they are feeling ill. Just like a human doctor, the veterinarian will examine the puppy and have a look at the eyes and stomach before treating him or giving advice to help him recover.

If your puppy is unwell, try to think how you like to be treated if you are sick. You might find that your pet wants to be left alone, or just wants gentle stroking. Your puppy may not want to play with you or join in your games. Try to keep him warm and go to the veterinarian if the puppy does not seem to be getting better or does not want to eat for more than a day.

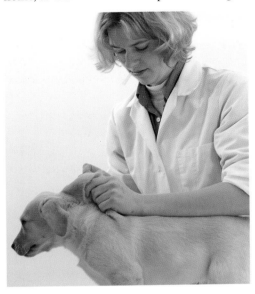

top: *A spaniel gets a general examination.*

left: *A nine-week-old Labrador puppy receives his primary vaccination in the back of the neck.*

right: *Make sure your puppy has a bowl of drinking water available at all times.*

how to know if your puppy is ill

- Your puppy does not want to eat
- Your puppy drinks more then normal
- Your puppy has an upset stomach or throws up
  - Your puppy acts very tired and does not want to move or play.

chocolate is bad

Chocolate is very harmful to dogs — even a small amount can poison a puppy. Chocolate-like treats sold especially for dogs are safe, because they are made with different ingredients.

puppy classes

Puppy classes are a great idea and can be fun for you and your puppy. The majority of good classes are happy to show you and your family how to train your pet easily using kindness.

Classes also give your puppy a chance to make friends with other dogs of a similar age — just like you do at school. Some classes even have sessions where the puppies are allowed off the leash to play with each other. Play times like this are very good for teaching your puppy how to behave with other dogs and to enjoy their company.

If you would like to take your puppy to a puppy class, your veterinarian may have a list of them that he or she recommends, or other dog owners in your neighborhood may know of a fun class nearby.

Most dog training schools accept puppies into a class as soon as they've had their vaccinations. Make sure your puppy is already used to wearing a collar and leash, and take some tasty treats to give as a reward when your puppy does well.

beds

All puppies need a bed of their own. This can be a plastic bed with a blanket in it, one made

left: *It may be fun to have your new puppy sleep in your bed with you, but remember — they grow bigger. Start as you mean to go on and make sure your dog sleeps in his own bed.*

collar and leash

It is essential that your puppy learns to wear a collar and leash. Make sure that these are light — nylon or leather are ideal. Do not use a chain collar or leash — they are too heavy and it may frighten him if the collar is pulled tight.

To begin with, your puppy may try to scratch the collar off. If you ignore this and play a game instead, he will soon forget about the collar.

exercise

All dogs need exercise. Not only does this keep them healthy, it also keeps their minds active and stimulated. The amount of exercise that your dog needs depends on its age and breed or type.

Puppies under the age of six months should

of soft fabric, a crate, or even a large cardboard box, but it should always be put somewhere where he can have peace and quiet without being disturbed.

Some puppies chew their beds or their bedding. Wicker baskets seem to be especially tempting, but they can also be harmful. Other types are usually better.

Make sure that your puppy sleeps in his bed and you sleep in yours! It may be fun to have your puppy in bed with you to begin with, but imagine what it would be like with a full-grown dog from one of the bigger breeds.

turning in circles

In the wild, dogs would dig their own den to lie in. Once this was done, the dog would turn around in the hole a few times to trample the surface down and to make himself comfortable. Your own puppy may do this before lying down, too.

above: *Make sure your puppy gets the right amount of exercise for his age. Thrown toys are ideal to get the puppy chasing about and learning to return them to you.*

have exercise little and often, but never so much that they are exhausted or overtired. After their first birthday, most dogs enjoy as much exercise as they can get, and all dogs need to go out for a walk at least once a day. This gives them the chance to see, hear, and smell different things — and to play with other dogs.

An enclosed or safe area where you can let your dog off the leash to run around and play is ideal, but you will need to teach your puppy to come back to you when you call.

left: *A collar may feel strange at first, but your puppy will soon get used to it.*

wearing a leash

Allow your puppy to walk around the house wearing the collar and trailing the leash behind. Pups have very sensitive necks, so never pull on the leash to make your puppy walk with you. If he is going in the opposite direction, simply stand still, then encourage him to come with you by offering a food treat or a toy. If your puppy continually pulls on the leash, you may want to use a gentle head-collar or body harness. These are comfortable to wear, as long as they are properly fitted, and are much kinder than collars that pull tight around the puppy's neck.

travel safety

Many puppies often throw up when they first travel in a vehicle. Most grow out of this quickly — especially once they realize that getting in a car means they will go to fun places! To make your pet calmer in a vehicle, put him in a traveling crate or encourage the puppy to lie down. Car harnesses are seat belts for dogs, making journeys safer.

puppy needs checklist
- Water ● Food ● Water bowl
- Food bowls (separate from yours)
- Brush and comb ● Collar and leash
- Bed or crate with blanket

learning **house** manners

immediately walk out of the room, and close the door. Ask an adult to help before you play with your puppy again.

Make it clear to the puppy that her bites hurt you.

mouthing

● Why do puppies bite things?

Most puppies try to chew anything and everything, and although this is normal behavior, it hurts if your puppy is chewing you! This is just what those teeth are for — your puppy is learning what is alive and what isn't.

If a dog bites a toy or stick, nothing happens, but if she bites you, you need to make it clear that it hurts. Puppies playing together bite each other's legs and tails, all in fun. However, if one bites too hard, the bitten playmate will let out a big yelp to tell the other puppy that he or she bit too hard.

● What you need to do

To teach your puppy that bites hurt, pretend that you are another puppy! Every time your dog tries to put her mouth on you, stand still, fold your arms and give a great big yelp. If your puppy stops and calms down, go back to play. If she becomes overexcited and does not calm down,

Parental Guide !

Mouthing is a normal part of puppy development. By teaching your puppy that there are unrewarding consequences to biting, her bites should gradually become softer and then stop altogether within a four- to six-week period. However, children need to learn to be calm and stop moving if the puppy is becoming overexcited. Isolating the puppy for a few moments will help.

Puppies soon learn that biting hurts!

dogs' teeth

Dogs have two sets of teeth, just like people. The first set, known as deciduous teeth, are the equivalent of a child's baby teeth. These become loose and gradually fall out by the time the puppy is about five months old. You may be lucky enough to find some of these baby teeth on the floor after your puppy has been chewing or playing.

The puppy's adult teeth come through very quickly. These are more rounded than the sharp, pointed baby teeth and are the dog's final set, which need to last a lifetime. Just like us, dogs need to have their teeth brushed if they are to be kept clean and healthy. Special toothbrushes and flavored toothpaste are made for this job.

house training

● Why do puppies use the house as a toilet?

Puppies need to learn where and when they can go to the toilet — and that means outdoors and not in the house! To begin with, puppies are just like babies and cannot be expected to have full control over their bodies — particularly at night — until they are about three to four months old. However, through careful training, puppies can quickly learn to be clean in the house.

● What you need to do

Your puppy will need to go to the toilet after playing, after waking up, after any kind of excitement — such as you coming home from school — and right after meals. At these times, take the puppy outside — the same place each time — and wait with her, even in the rain. Gently repeating some words, like "Be quick," helps your puppy to remember why you are both outside.

As soon as your puppy starts to sniff around, or circle, give gentle praise. Once she has been to the toilet, give lots of praise and a special food treat as a reward.

If your puppy does not go to the toilet, bring her back inside, but keep a careful watch. Sure signs are sniffing and circling around, looking for a place to use. If you cannot watch all the time, put the puppy in a crate or playpen, or in an enclosed area where an accident can be easily cleaned.

If you catch your puppy about to go to the toilet in your house, say "Outside" in an urgent voice, then take her quickly outside to show her where she should go — even if it's too late!

Never, ever be angry with your puppy if she has an accident in the house. It simply means that you weren't quick enough!

"Oops!"

jumping up

● Why do puppies jump up?

As you probably know, puppies jump up at you to be friendly! They love to get as close to your face as possible and some even try to get onto your knee when you sit down.

Jumping up may be fine if you are wearing old clothes and don't mind muddy paws all over you, but if you teach your puppy that it's alright to jump up at you, she may do it to other people too. This can be a nuisance, or even dangerous if your puppy was to knock someone over.

● What you need to do

Think about what you would prefer your puppy to do when she greets you and your friends. How about sitting, or fetching a toy? While you are teaching your puppy to do this instead, make sure that jumping up of any kind is ignored. Turn your back and fold your arms if she jumps up, but praise and stroke her if your pet is sitting or being calm.

Next, ask a friend to help. Hold your puppy on the leash, or ask an adult to hold the leash for you. When your friends arrive, ask them to ignore your puppy completely to begin with. Look at the sky, the trees, or the ceiling, but not at the puppy — until she has calmed down! Your friends should give praise as soon as your puppy sits or lies down, but must instantly stand up and turn away again if the puppy jumps up.

Dogs may jump up at you to be friendly, but this could knock someone over or cause an accident.

Dogs love to get as close to you as they can, but face licking should be discouraged — it may not please your friends or other visitors to your house.

chewing

● Why do puppies chew things?

Dogs need to chew! Puppies particularly need to chew while their second set of teeth are growing through, since it helps to ease the discomfort from their gums.

Sadly, dogs do not know the difference between a stick and a piece of furniture, nor an old slipper and a brand new shoe. If you do not give your puppy enough things of her own to chew, she will happily chew your things!

● What you need to do

Give your dog lots of safe chew-toys. Toys such as Kongs are designed specially so that they can be stuffed with food. Small pieces of food fall out while the dog is chewing, which will really keep your pet happy!

Digging comes naturally to dogs, so encourage your puppy to dig where it won't damage your yard.

digging

● Why do puppies dig?

Digging is not only a normal dog behavior from a puppy's point of view, it's fun, too! For some breeds, such as terriers, it's a truly natural thing to do. In the wild, dogs dig for many reasons: to find prey hidden underground, to scratch for roots to eat, to bury food, to create a shallow hole to sleep in, and for the protection of young puppies in the den. Many puppies also dig for fun if they are bored!

A bark can mean many different things. This 12-week-old Terrier-Collie cross, wants to have his toy thrown.

● What you need to do

Ask an adult to help you make a digging pit for your puppy somewhere in the yard. Dig a hole, then fill the hole with soil mixed with coarse sand, so that water will drain away and your puppy won't become too muddy.

Let your puppy watch you dig in the hole and bury something wonderful at the bottom, such as a bone, dog chew, or toy. Allow your puppy to dig up the object and play with it. Over the next few weeks and months, keep hiding objects in the hole. The idea is that if your puppy's digging is rewarded in this area, she won't bother digging anywhere else.

barking

● Why do puppies bark?

Dogs bark for a number of reasons: to raise the alarm about intruders, to call the rest of their "pack," to show fear or loneliness, and as a display of aggression to keep animals or people away. Many dogs also bark in sheer excitement.

● What you need to do

Make sure that you are not accidentally encouraging your dog to bark. Some people laugh or praise their puppy when she first barks at the door, or when playing, and this means that the puppy will probably do it again. Other owners shout at their dogs when they bark, and this makes the dog think that her owner is barking encouragement.

Keep calm and quiet when your puppy is barking and she will have to do the same to listen to you. An interesting toy can stop a bored or lonely puppy from barking.

It's all chew toys to them! Give puppies appropriate things to chew and they will leave your things alone.

stealing items

● **Why do puppies steal things?**

For fun! Just like you, puppies love to have fun, and if they discover that stealing your things gets attention, they will do it as much as they can. Some puppies like to steal items and run off with them, either to chew them, or just to see what will happen. This could be dangerous if your puppy swallows the object, and it can be very annoying if she chews your favorite toys, books, or shoes.

● **What you need to do**

Make sure that your puppy cannot get to your most precious things — so pick them up and put them out of reach. Puppies especially love socks, pens, and shoes. If your puppy picks up something that she is not meant to have, do not chase her, because this will make it an even bigger game. Instead, call your puppy and give her praise and a food treat in return for the stolen item.

stealing food

Some puppies learn to steal food from people's plates or hands while they are eating. Make sure that you are the only one to eat your food, and do not give your puppy treats while you are eating.

types of bark

The way that your puppy barks can tell you what she is thinking and feeling. For example, one single, gruff "woof" is known as an "alarm bark." This sound is used to tell other members of the dog's pack or family that there is danger around. Dogs often bark like this if they are feeling a little frightened — if they hear a noise outside, for example. If this happens, just ignore your puppy until she settles down again.

A quick succession of barks usually means "keep away." Dogs may bark at other dogs like this, or at people, if they are fearful or feel threatened. Dogs also bark with joy and excitement. This is normally higher pitched than other types of barking and is often mixed with whimpering and whining.

Occasionally, dogs howl because they are feeling lonely. Some hounds, such as the Basset Hound and the Bloodhound, are more likely to howl than bark if they are excited.

companionship,
security, and **respect**

Dogs need companionship — which is what makes them such good pets. In the wild, dogs live in groups that are called packs. Living together like this means that they can hunt large prey to eat by working as a team, and gain warmth, security, and friendship from each other.

When puppies are born in a wild dog pack or a wolf pack, many adult dogs help with their care and safety. This is just like having aunts and uncles that care for you.

Most pet dogs are kept in homes where they are the only dog, so your puppy will rely on the human members of the family for companionship and fun. In homes with more than one dog, you need to work extra hard to make sure that you spend time with all the dogs separately, building up a friendship between you and each of them. This makes sure that they don't just rely on each other.

time with your dog

It is very important that you spend time with your puppy, concentrating on building a friendship and training. Imagine if you have a friend who ignores you all the time, or only wants to watch TV or sit in front of the computer, rather than playing — you wouldn't be friends for very long! Puppies need training, play, and companionship. If your puppy gets a little of each from you every day, he will be happy to settle down and watch TV, too.

time out

Just as important as spending time with your puppy is spending some time apart. This happens anyway when you go to school or are out with friends, but sometimes at home you need to concentrate on homework or play with one of your human friends, rather than your puppy. This is fine as spending time away from each other is good for your puppy, too.

In the first few weeks and months, your puppy will need lots of sleep. This means that he needs to have a bed or place to go and rest quietly,

without being disturbed. Dogs can become irritable and upset if they are being pestered all the time, so make sure you and your puppy have enough time out.

respect

The best friendships are based on respect. This means that you are kind to each other and understand that sometimes you do not agree! Puppies need respect, and they need to learn to respect you, too.

You also need to have some rules about your behavior toward your puppy. Pushing, pulling, pinching, smacking, and shouting are out! If your puppy is annoying you, take some time out and do something else. Ask an adult for help if you are unsure what to do, especially if the puppy seems to be in a bad mood. Dogs cannot tell us when they are feeling unwell or are just too tired to play nicely. Be patient with your puppy — we all have good and bad days.

Some dogs enjoy close contact and boisterous games, but give your pup some peace and quiet, too.

play

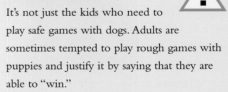

Puppies love to play. If you watch dogs playing with each other, you will see that they play in ways that are different to us. Dogs don't use hands to hold bats, throw balls, or move a computer mouse. Instead, they use their mouths, their paws, and their whole bodies. This means that puppies need to understand that they have to play differently with us than they do with other dogs.

Many puppies are encouraged to play rough–and–tumble games on the floor by their owners. This can be a big mistake. Allowing your dog to bite your arms and legs in play when she is a puppy may seem funny, but what happens when your puppy gets older? It is never right for a dog to bite a person, so it is unfair to expect your pet to understand that she can bite you in play but cannot bite another child in the same way. Many dogs get into trouble for biting people — don't allow yours to be one of them.

There are plenty of other games that you can play with your puppy that are great fun and also safe (*see pages 82 to 89*). Make sure that you show everyone how much you care for your puppy by playing these types of games, not rough ones.

Parental Guide

It's not just the kids who need to play safe games with dogs. Adults are sometimes tempted to play rough games with puppies and justify it by saying that they are able to "win."

If you are unsure about the kind of games your family plays with the dog, ask yourself one question: Would it be acceptable for your dog to start the same game with a four-year-old in the park?

If you think the child or their parent would be frightened, or the dog uses her mouth on a human in any way — STOP! Find more suitable games to play instead.

noise

Some puppies are quiet, some love to bark. If you have a puppy that gets over-excited and becomes noisy, don't be tempted to join in with him by shouting or screaming! Instead, stop the game for a few minutes until your puppy calms down, then try again.

keeping clean

Dogs are generally clean in their habits. They do not like to be dirty and always prefer to go to the toilet well away from any area where they eat or sleep.

There are a few illnesses that a puppy can give to a person, and even some that can be passed from person to puppy. These are easily avoided by following sensible rules:

- Always wash your hands before eating
- If you have played with your dog outdoors, wash your hands when you come in
- Keep your food dishes and plates separate from your pup's
- Do not allow your dog to lick your face or your food!

Parental Guide

The risks to human health from dogs that are kept free from parasites are minimal. Basic, sensible hygiene precautions will keep your family safe. Ensure that your dog is regularly treated for worms and fleas and clean up all droppings from your yard immediately. A few children suffer from hair allergies; take the advice of your doctor if you are concerned about this.

sequence: *This 12-week-old Lurcher pup is younger and smaller than her playmate, a Labrador-Golden Retriever-cross, but she gives as good as she gets. It may look rough, but these puppies are having fun.*

socialization

Imagine if you never went out of your home, never went to school, and never played with your friends. Life would be pretty miserable! For some puppies this is what life can be like until they come to live in their new home. Suddenly they are surrounded by new things: the television, the sounds of people, the

Puppies and young dogs need to meet all kinds of unusual things — and lots of different people…

sight of traffic, and the smells of other animals. Think what a shock this must be.

To make sure that your puppy is confident, friendly, and relaxed around people, other dogs, and all the sights and sounds of your neighborhood, it is important that your pup meets them on a regular basis. Puppies need to see as many things as possible in the outside world before they are too old, otherwise they may be frightened of them later on.

This means you have some exciting work to do. Every day your puppy needs to meet someone or something new. These things may be in the home, like hearing the washing machine working, or they might be outside, like meeting another dog or watching you ride your bike.

Always make sure your puppy is safe; a bad experience can be worse than none at all.

socializing at home

If your puppy hasn't had all his vaccinations yet, don't worry, there is still a lot that you can do. Ask your friends' parents if you can visit their homes with your puppy, and invite your friends around to meet the new pet if your parents approve. Your puppy can meet your friends' dogs, as long as they are friendly and have had their vaccinations.

socialization checklist

See how many of these things your puppy can meet in one week.

Inside the home

- Hearing and seeing the washing machine or dryer while it's on
- Hearing and seeing the vacuum cleaner
- Hearing the telephone
- Hearing and seeing the television
- Hearing people talking to each other
- Hearing people singing
- Watching visitors arriving and leaving

Inside and outside

- Meeting men and women
- Meeting a man with a beard
- Meeting a person wearing glasses
- Meeting a person wearing a hat
- Meeting a person wearing a crash helmet
- Meeting a person who walks using a cane or a walker
- Meeting a person with an umbrella
- Meeting five different girls and boys

Meeting other dogs

- Meeting large or small adult dogs
- Meeting black or brown adult dogs
- Meeting yellow or white adult dogs
- Meeting another puppy

…and learn to cope with all kinds of unexpected situations.

Meeting other animals

- Meeting a horse
- Meeting a cat
- Meeting any other animals

Travel

- Automobile travel
- Going on a bus
- Going on a train or subway
- Going on a boat

Outdoors

- Seeing baby strollers or shopping carts
- Seeing a tractor or truck
- Going to a grassy area (like a park or field)
- Visiting a pedestrian area (shopping mall or local stores)
- Going for a walk along the street
- Visiting a different home or yard

- Going inside a store where dogs are allowed
- Standing outside a supermarket (but do not leave your puppy tied up alone)

no comfort

Sometimes puppies can be frightened when they first meet something new. Although it is tempting to cuddle your puppy to make him feel better, wait until he is feeling brave, then stroke and give praise. The more people and dogs your puppy meets, the braver he will be. Your pet will enjoy going with you and will be as pleased to see your friends as you are.

meeting other dogs

Your puppy needs to meet lots of other dogs while he is still young, to learn their

These nine puppies are all eight weeks old, but see how different they are from each other. Try to imagine what it would be like if you were one of them meeting any of the other eight. They have all been photographed with the same squeaky boot toy for size comparison.

Saluki Lurcher

English Springer Spaniel

Cavalier-Spitz cross

Border Collie

Yorkshire Terrier

"language" and enjoy playing with them. Different breeds and types of dogs probably look very strange to your puppy at first. Over time, your puppy will discover that other dog breeds look, sound, smell, and even behave in different ways, but that they are all still dogs!

Think about how that tiny Yorkshire Terrier you can see below must feel when he first meets the German Shepherd Dog, who is four-and-a-half times bigger!

Some dogs even sound different — Basenjis and some other breeds do not bark, but make an unusual yodeling sound.

Some dogs have upright ears, others have drop ears.

Tails give a lot of information about how a dog is feeling, but can look very different, too. Compare a Golden Retriever's flowing mane of a tail to a Pug's little stub.

Sometimes, it's the length and type of coat that needs some getting used to. At either end of the hair extremes are the Old English Sheepdog — almost a walking rug — and the Mexican Hairless Dog, which, as its name implies, is completely bald.

And some dogs may not look like any other breed at all, like the exotic Lhasa Apso, Chow, and Shar Pei.

meeting on the leash

When you are outside, try to let your puppy off the leash to meet other dogs, if it is in a safe area, or on a loose leash. If the leash is tight, your puppy could easily feel intimidated by the other dog because he cannot get away from the other dog. Your pet may also associate the discomfort around the neck with meeting another dog.

German Shepherd Dog

Schnauzer

Cavalier King Charles Spaniel

Patterdale-Jack Russell Terrier cross

handling your puppy

stroking your puppy

Most puppies love being stroked and petted. However, the way that you do this is very important. Imagine being patted on the top of *your* head all day. It would not be very enjoyable — it might even give you a headache!

Instead, puppies love to be stroked gently, usually on the chest and belly. Use the tips of your fingers when tickling your puppy and the flat of your hand for gentle stoking. Stop immediately if the puppy starts to wriggle or

Handling your puppy all over is essential.

tries to put her mouth on you.

Many puppies offer you the part that they want you to stroke — very often this is the rump or belly. See if you can get your puppy to roll over so that you can stroke her belly.

Watch carefully to see where your puppy likes being stroked the best, then choose that place when you want to give her attention.

Try these ways of stroking to find out where your puppy likes being tickled:

1. Tickle the puppy on the chest area between the front legs and watch closely. If she enjoys this, she will stay still or move closer to you.
2. Now stroke her shoulders and sides. Does the puppy wriggle and try to get away? If so, your pet may prefer to be stroked somewhere else.
3. Try stroking your puppy's back. Most puppies do not like having their faces, heads, or tails stroked, so offer a food treat while you touch these places.

puppy's body weight is back on the ground. Puppies sometimes try to jump when they see that the floor is close and this can cause an accident if you do not have a firm hold.

safe holding

Many puppies do not like being picked up, or being held close. Do not pick up your puppy unless you really have to, and only if there is an adult there to help you. Puppies can wriggle and jump out of your arms very easily and hurt themselves, so be very careful.

It is very important that the puppy feels safe and her whole weight is supported:

1. Place one hand up underneath the puppy's chest, cradling this area and putting your fingers between her front legs.
2. Your other hand should then scoop the puppy from underneath and support her bottom (*see the picture, above right*).
3. The puppy can then be lifted onto a surface, your lap, or if you are carrying your pet, tucked well into your chest.

Particular care needs to be taken when putting the puppy down again. Make sure that you keep a firm hold until you can feel that the

holding your puppy
Are you…?

4 to 7 years old Do not try to pick up your puppy — ask an adult to do it for you

7 to 10 years old Only pick up your puppy with an adult to help you

10 to 14 years old Only pick up your puppy if you really need to — follow the "safe holding" rules very carefully

Parental Guide

Dropping a puppy or holding her in a way that causes discomfort or distress can result in irreparable physical and emotional damage to your puppy and potentially, to your child. Encourage your children to groom and examine the puppy on the floor or, with your help, after carefully lifting your dog onto a non-slip surface.

how to examine your puppy

Examining your puppy every day will mean that you will be the first to notice if she is not well, or has a cut or scratch. An inspection like this prepares her for visits to the veterinarian. You can even listen to your puppy's heart if you have a toy stethoscope!

keeping a puppy still

No matter how wriggly your puppy is, you should never grab her skin, hair, or tail to keep her still. Holding the collar or leash is the best way to keep the dog still if you need to. Remember that the collar fits around your puppy's neck — a sensitive area. It can hurt your puppy if you yank on the leash or drag her by the collar, too, so use a food treat or toy to encourage your pet to come to you or to move around.

Examine your puppy carefully every day to check on her health.

important

In these pictures of Peter examining his puppy, it is his mom who lifted the puppy onto the table. On his own, Peter would keep the pup on the floor.

Examining the front paws.

Examining the teeth.

inspect your puppy from head to toe

1. With your puppy standing, look into each eye. Use a toy or food treat if you need to distract her.

2. Move onto your dog's ears. Move the ear flap away from the head and look right down the ear canal. Give praise if your puppy stays calm.

3. Lift your pup's lips, first one side, then the other, to allow both sides of the mouth to be seen. Then open her mouth very gently to see the tongue and throat. Be very gentle. Give praise and a special treat for good

Examining the ears.

Opening the mouth to look at the tongue.

Examining the eyes.

Examining the hind paws.

behavior.

4. Move on to the neck and shoulders. Feel every inch of the puppy's skin and coat, moving gently down the front of each leg. Lift the front feet one at a time to look at your dog's nails, then tuck her foot under and examine the bottom of the foot, and you will see the pads.

5. Moving back up to the shoulders, run your hands down your puppy's coat to the hips, and then down to your pup's ribs. Can you feel them?

6. Feel down each hind or back leg, then inside the thighs. Lift each rear foot, one at a time, and have a good look at them, as you did the front ones.

7. Finally, stroke down the whole of your puppy's body, from the head to the tip of the tail.

Be calm and very gentle while you are examining your puppy. Give special treats throughout for your puppy being good, and play a game with her with a toy when you are finished.

grooming your puppy

what grooming is for

Grooming your puppy is as important as you taking a shower. Dogs needs to be groomed regularly to prevent their coat becoming matted, skin becoming unhealthy, and their smelling unpleasant. Dogs' skin produces oils to keep their hair in good, waterproof condition, but this can become smelly if the coat is not kept clean.

Just like us, dogs also feel better when they are clean and tidy. Even short-coated dogs need regular brushing. All dogs need

All dogs need grooming, but long-haired breeds need more regular attention.

their ears cleaned, teeth brushed and nails kept tidy — as well as to take a bath sometimes!

how to groom your puppy

Brushing

Make sure that the brush you use suits your dog's coat and skin. Brush gently, in the direction the hair grows. With long hair, use downward, sweeping movements. Do not tug or pull if you find a mat or knot, but gently ease it free with the comb or ask an adult to help you loosen it.

With your puppy standing up, hold a treat as a distraction and use your other hand to brush all over the dog's body. Praise him all the time for good behavior. After a few grooming sessions you should be able to brush your pup without using a treat, but always give one after brushing as a reward for good behavior.

Combing

Use a comb for fine hair around the face and ears. Be very careful not to scratch your puppy's skin or eyes.

Cleaning ears

Your puppy's ears should be regularly cleaned by wiping the underside of the ear flap and visible parts with a soft tissue, or dampened cotton ball if necessary. Never push anything into the ear — even a small cotton ball or swab could cause damage to the dog's ear drum and hearing. If you find brown gunk in the ear or if the ear smells bad, the dog may have an ear infection. Tell an adult that your puppy needs to be taken to a veterinarian.

types of brushes

Lots of different types of brushes are suitable for grooming your puppy. The type you need depends on the length of your puppy's coat, but it's most important that the brush is comfortable for your pet. Rubber brushes are ideal. These massage your puppy, as well as brush the hair and remove dead hair from the coat. If you are unsure about whether a new brush will be gentle on your puppy's skin, try it on your own head first!

cleaning teeth

Just like us, dogs should have clean teeth. Cleaning the teeth is not difficult if he gets used to it early. Specially designed dog toothpaste has the right ingredients — it doesn't foam up or taste minty, but is often flavored to taste like chicken or liver!

You can put a little toothpaste on one finger or use a finger brush — a toothbrush for dogs that fits on a person's finger. Rub your finger or fingerbrush gently on his teeth and gums, working from front to back and brushing from the gum to the tooth. This gets pieces of food from between the teeth and massages the gums.

Clean the teeth for only a few seconds until he is used to it, and make sure you give him a reward when you have finished for

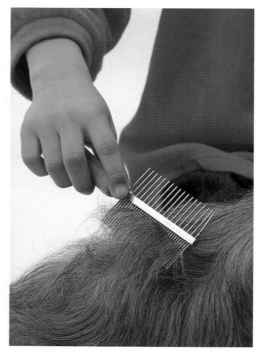

*A brush, **above**, and a comb, **right**, do different jobs when grooming dogs, just as they do with human hair. In the center you can see a variety of combs and brushes.*

left: *Pups keep their teeth clean by chewing. Make sure that the chew toy is fun and safe — bones are dangerous if they splinter.*

right: *Take care to dry your puppy all over. Just like humans, a damp puppy can catch a chill.*

taking a bath

Unlike us, most dogs only need a bath a few times a year, unless they get particularly muddy or smelly! Bathing some dogs too often may damage the coat.

To bathe your puppy, you will need the following equipment:

- An adult to help with lifting and holding
- A tub or basin, depending on your puppy's size
- Pet shampoo specially designed for dogs
- Warm water and a plastic pitcher or shower attachment with spray nozzle to rinse the puppy clean
- Lots of old towels to help get your puppy dry
- Brush and comb, to make sure the puppy really looks tidy at the end.

Most dogs do not like being bathed as it is not natural for them — wild dogs may swim and paddle, but none have shampoo. You

being calm and quiet. Eventually the dog will let you clean all his teeth at one time.

dog hair

A dog's coat is made of hair, not fur. The only large areas where dogs do not have hair is inside their hind legs, their mouths, and on the bottoms of their foot pads. Some dogs have very hairy ears that may need to be trimmed.

no hair!

A few dog breeds are born without any hair at all! These "naked" dogs were originally born as an accident of nature. Such dogs as the Chinese Crested need protection from the sun and cold, and often have pimples on their skin.

coat that could irritate the puppy's skin. When the coat is free of shampoo and foam, ask an adult to lift him out of the bath.

Now you can get to work with the towel to get your puppy dry. Watch out for the shaking, though. Some people say that dogs only shake water from their coat when their heads get wet, so try washing the head last.

drying your puppy

It's very important that your puppy is properly dried after a bath, or he might catch a chill. If the weather is warm, you can take the dog outside to be toweled dry, then play a game to keep him warm. Some dogs love the feel of the hair dryer but others hate it. Never use a hair dryer on a dog that does not like it — it just means you will need to do more work with the towel!

below: *That's better! All wrapped up, snug and warm, it looks like it's time for a nap!*

need to be very calm and patient when you give your puppy a bath, but expect to get just as wet as the dog!

Make sure your puppy is wet all over before using shampoo. Put some shampoo in a bowl with some warm water, then pour it over him and rub it in. Don't get shampoo or water in your pet's eyes and ears — we all know how much it can hurt if shampoo gets in our eyes.

Your puppy will need a thorough rinse in clean, warm water. Make sure the water runs clear, as it is easy to leave suds in the

giving attention

does your puppy need attention?

Puppies need attention to build friendship with their human families and to learn how to behave around other people. Attention means looking at your puppy, talking to and touching her, and playing together. Always try to give attention for good behavior and ignore behavior that you don't like.

looking at your puppy

Even looking at your puppy gives her attention. See if you can make the dog's tail wag just by looking and smiling! This means that if your puppy is being good, you can give a reward just by looking at him or her. If the puppy is doing something you don't like, such as jumping up, turn your whole face away from her.

above: *Watch your puppy carefully while you are giving him attention — is he enjoying it?*

right: *For your puppy, being ignored is just as important as learning to have fun together!*

talking to you puppy

Most dogs love the sound of their owner's voice, even if they don't know what is being said. Dogs do not understand English, but they do respond to the way you speak. Try speaking in a very soft, gentle voice to your puppy and see how much your puppy enjoys it. Dogs probably think that their owners are barking at them if they shout!

touching your puppy

Practice handling your puppy (*see page 40*) so that you know where the dog likes to be touched. Do not give attention by touching a puppy anywhere she feels uncomfortable. Gentle stroking on your pup's chest and belly are usually favorites.

doing something you don't like, such as jumping up.

Ignoring your puppy may sound mean, but it is a very useful way of telling a dog that she is not behaving well. For example, if your puppy is barking for attention while you are trying to concentrate on your schoolwork or talking to a friend on the phone, it might be tempting to tell the puppy to stop or even to shout. Because dogs do not understand words, what will your puppy think is happening? You looked, talked to, and maybe even touched her — so you must be pleased with her behavior! Because it got attention, the puppy will probably do the same thing again and again in the future.

Instead, ignoring bad behavior tells a dog that you don't like what she is doing and you are not going to give any attention if she does the same bad thing again.

when should you give attention?

Try to give attention when you have time and can concentrate just on your puppy. If you try giving attention while dressing or playing with your friends, you might accidentally give the puppy attention for

how to ignore your puppy

1. Using all your acting skills, turn your back to your puppy as if you can't see her.
2. Fold your arms, so the puppy cannot nudge you or reach you.
3. Look away, at the ceiling or the sky, so you aren't giving attention by looking at the puppy.
4. Keep perfectly quiet or, if you are talking to another person, continue your conversation.
5. As soon as your puppy stops the behavior you didn't like, you can turn back again and pretend nothing ever happened!

playing with your puppy

toys are chewed, they must be more fun to play with than your toys.

Kong toys top your puppy's chew toy "wish list." These are rubber toys shaped like a small cone. They are hollow inside so they can be stuffed full of deliciousfood treats to lick and eat.

If you get really good at filling a Kong toy, your puppy will spend a long time chewing on it to get all the tasty bits of food out. The food rewards the pup for chewing the toy, making the Kong far more interesting than any of your toys.

If you do not have a Kong toy, safe, hollow bones and plastic bottles can be filled with biscuits and treats for your pup to work on.

above and **below:** *A nine-week-old puppy plays with a Kong that has been stuffed with treats.*

There are lots of ways you can play with your puppy. Puppies are full of energy and yours will love the attention he is given when you play together — and it's just as much fun for you!

Most games you can play with a dog need a toy of some kind. There are many toys that your puppy can play with safely — the main types are chew toys, tug toys, and balls. Some need to be bought from a pet store, but others you can make yourself.

chew toys

Chew toys are any toys that your puppy can safely chew on and play with alone. To your puppy, shoes, furniture, and your toys are all chew toys! To make sure that only your dog's

above: *A Kong stuffed full of cheese and other treats is irresistible to playful puppies.*

recipe for a stuffed toy

1. Squash some soft cheese right inside the Kong or hollow toy. Your puppy will be able to smell it through the small hole at the end of the Kong.

2. Smear some peanut butter, meat or fish paste, spread all around the inside for your puppy to lick.

3. Pack in some large dog biscuits. Push these in really hard, so they will be tough for the puppy to get out.

4. Add a little more moist food or cheese, to hold it all together, and then some small pieces of dog food that will fall out easily.

5. Give to your puppy, sit back, and watch TV uninterrupted!

left: *This 11-week-old puppy has just discovered the joys of the toy box. The toys around this page are suitable for your puppy to play with under supervision.*

tug toys

Tug toys are for you and your dog to play with together, with an adult nearby to help. Cotton ropes, balls on ropes, and twisted rope

toys are ideal.
Most puppies love to
grab a toy, chase it, and
pull on it with you. These
games are safe and fun as long as you and the
dog both play by the rules:

above: *Tug games should always be supervised, especially when young children play.*

people rules for tug games — you promise...

1. To only play tug games when an adult is there to help.
2. To be fun and exciting, but not to shout or scream.
3. To quickly drag the toy along the floor, to get your pet interested, rather than pushing it in the dog's face.
4. To teach your puppy to let go of the toy without a struggle
5. To hold the toy lower than your waist all the time you are playing.
6. Not to jerk your puppy's head or do anything that could hurt him.

dog rules for tug games

1. Your dog must **never** put its mouth on you or your clothes when playing. If he does, the game must stop immediately.
2. Your dog will let go of the toy right away when you ask in a quiet voice (*see opposite*).
3. Your dog will keep all four feet on the ground when playing and will not jump at you.
4. Your dog will have fun and will calm down right after playing.

above: *Squeaky toys are good fun — especially for Terrier dogs!*

making tug games safe and fun

Dogs love to chase toys, and this is the fun behind a good game of tug. To get your puppy to play, move the toy along the ground around your feet in front of him, as if the toy was alive and trying to run away. When your puppy chases after it, see if you can be quicker, until he grabs it.

Once the puppy has grabbed the toy, give a few gentle tugs. Stop immediately and walk away if your puppy growls or grabs you instead of the toy. After a quick play, offer the puppy a really tasty treat instead of the toy. Hold the toy when the dog drops it to eat the food, but do not snatch it away. Have another game when your puppy has finished with the treat.

Repeat this several times, then say "Give!" or "Drop!" quietly, just before you offer the treat. Your puppy will quickly learn that the word means "drop the toy and wait for a treat." After a few games you will not need to use the food treat, since having another game is a good enough reward.

Parental Guide

IMPORTANT! Tug games are only safe if the dog has been taught to let go of the toy without a struggle on a single, quiet command. Tug games should always be supervised carefully and should be stopped immediately if the child or puppy is getting over-excited. If your child is very young or the dog is boisterous or large, encourage other kinds of games, such as Hide and Seek the toy.

safety first!

Sticks are not safe for dogs to play with and you should never throw them for your puppy to fetch. Sticks can badly injure a dog's mouth and throat, so use rubber toys instead.

Balls can be fun, but make sure that they are larger than a tennis ball. A tennis ball or anything smaller could be swallowed or get stuck in your dog's throat.

Squeaky toys are enjoyable for dogs, especially terriers, but make sure that your puppy does not pull the toy apart and swallow the part that makes the squeaky sound.

games to play with your puppy

Soccer

Soccer can be really fun to play with your dog. Make sure you use a ball that the puppy cannot accidentally puncture with his teeth, and use one that's too large for your dog to pick up. Be careful how you kick the ball — do not kick it toward your puppy — and encourage him to push the ball back toward you with its nose. See page 86 for help on how to teach your dog to push a ball with his nose or feet.

Frisbee

Some dogs become expert Frisbee catchers! This takes a lot of time and skill to teach. To begin with, train your pup to simply run and fetch the Frisbee when you throw it. Only later, when the dog is fully grown, can you teach your pet to jump in the air to catch the Frisbee in mid-flight.

Hide and Seek

Hide and Seek is an excellent game to play, and is fun with just yourself and your puppy, or with friends. First, teach your puppy to sit or lie down and stay (*see page 64*).

While your puppy is "staying," run and hide, in the home or the yard. When you are hidden, call your puppy, but only once. Your dog now has to hunt for you! When you are found, reward with a pat and a food treat so your puppy will be eager to play again.

"Pass, please!" Soccer is not only good exercise for your puppy, it is also good for obedience training.

With maturity and practice, many dogs make excellent Frisbee-catchers. Never aim the Frisbee toward your puppy— throw it away from you and let the him chase after it.

games to avoid

Rough-and-tumble games and any play where the puppy grabs you or your clothes, or growls, are definitely out! These may seem fun at first, but think how much trouble they could get you and him into when you have a fully grown dog. Play safe!

Do not allow your puppy to chase you. If you are running and your puppy tries to run up behind you, grab your clothing, or bite at your feet, stand still. Although being chased is fun at first, your puppy will soon be larger and stronger. Most adult dogs could easily outrun you and even trip you or knock you over. Worse, your dog may do this to another child when you are at the park, which could get you and your pet into serious trouble.

Never chase your puppy, either — especially if he has stolen something. If you give chase, your puppy will learn that stealing things starts a great game and will do it more and more. Puppies can even learn to hide objects from their owners, or defend things, and again, this can cause trouble later on.

Even puppies as young as nine weeks old can be taught to retrieve a toy.

feeding your puppy

Just like us, puppies enjoy eating their favorite foods. However, food that we like should not be given to dogs, because it can upset their stomachs. There are lots of different types and flavors of food specially made for dogs. You only need to look at the rows of cans, packets, and sacks on store shelves to see how much choice there is.

At first you should feed the puppy the same type of food as she was given by the breeder — the owner of the puppy's mother. Changing the type of food suddenly can cause a stomach upset.

Dogs don't really care what their food looks like, as long as it smells and tastes good! Dogs are happy to be fed the same kind of food each day — in fact it is better that they have the same food, since their stomachs can be sensitive.

Can you tell what is in the food you are giving your puppy? Probably not! Dog food is usually cooked and packaged so that the ingredients cannot be seen. It's important that the food is of good quality, and doesn't just look and smell meaty. You can sometimes tell what is in dog food by reading the food packaging — chicken, lamb, and turkey are easy to digest, so it's good if they are the main ingredients.

how to feed

Each puppy needs to have her own dish for meals. This can be plastic, stainless steel, or ceramic (pottery). Some puppies get very excited and run around or even bark while their owner is getting their dinner ready. Try to keep your puppy calm by giving her the "sit" and "stay" commands (*see pages 64 and 67*) until the food is ready.

vegetarian dogs?

Dogs can be fed a vegetarian diet but it needs to be carefully formulated to make sure the vegetables have all the vitamins and minerals that a dog needs to stay fit and healthy. In the wild, dogs eat a lot of plants, roots, and berries, as well as insects and meat from prey they have caught.

Sit! Wait!

Dogs love dinner! But it is good obedience training to make them sit and wait for it, as illustrated in this sequence: "Sit, Wait — Okay!"

above: *A Border Collie pup eats from his food bowl, with a water bowl nearby.*
below: *That's a large bowl for a small puppy, but she will soon grow into it!*

above: *These two pups eat nicely from the same bowl, but it's unusual — two puppies eating from the same bowl are more likely to squabble, like these* **below***.*

how much food?

The amount of food a puppy needs depends on her size. A large breed, such as a Mastiff, needs much more food than a smaller breed, such as a Yorkshire Terrier. The best way to tell if you are feeding the right amount is to feel your dog's sides. If you can feel her ribs, but cannot see them, the puppy is around the right weight. If you cannot feel the ribs you may need to give your pet less food and make sure she gets more exercise.

how often?

How often you need to feed your puppy depends on her age. Most puppies are fed four meals every day when they are very young. By the time they are around 14 weeks old, most puppies are fed three times a day.

For most adult dogs, two meals a day is ideal. This means that they don't get too hungry in the daytime and they don't eat too much, either!

Wait!

Okay!

preventing food guarding

Some puppies can be protective over their food. They may growl or even snap if someone comes too close to their dinner while they are eating. If this happens with your puppy, immediately walk away and tell an adult.

Usually, puppies only protect their food because they are worried that someone will take it away. To make sure that your puppy enjoys having you around at her mealtimes, follow the suggestions below:

1. Put the food bowl on the floor with nothing in it. Your puppy will probably look in it, then look at you.
2. Put one spoonful of dog food in the dish and let your puppy eat it.
3. Keep adding a spoonful then letting the puppy eat it until the whole meal has been eaten.

Your puppy will soon realize that you are the food fairy — the one that gives food — not the food monster, who tries to take it away!

Once your puppy is happy with this, move onto the next stage:

1. Put food in the dish. Place it on the floor and let the puppy start eating.
2. From a distance, gently throw a piece of tasty food and see if you can get it in the dish.
3. Let your puppy eat the treat, no matter where it lands, then let her finish the food in the bowl.
4. Three or four times a week, throw or drop a food treat in the dish while she is eating.

To prevent food guarding, Emily puts food pellets into this nine-week-old's dish while he is eating.

food treats

Treats are small, tasty bits of food that are
useful in training when you want to reward
your dog. When you are at home, you can
easily use pieces of food as rewards that your
pet would have had for dinner. This way the
puppy will also not put on too much weight.

When you are at a training class or outside,
you will need to have more tasty food to
keep your dog interested. Tiny pieces of
cooked chicken, cooked liver, or even hot
dog usually work well.

Teach your puppy to take food treats gently.

taking treats

Teach the puppy to be gentle by only
allowing the food to be taken if your dog does
not use teeth. Use the command "off" or
"leave" (*see page 72*) if you need to. Most dogs
learn to be very gentle — but if yours isn't,
ask an adult for help.

how to give treats

Keep your treats in a dog-proof container.
Take them out one at a time and hold them
between thumb and fingers. If your puppy
tries to snatch the food, you may prefer to
drop it onto the floor to let the dog eat it, or
to put the treat on the palm of your hand.
Then you can hold your hand out flat, as if
you were feeding a horse.

*Puppies often regulate their own daily intake of food —
but most will clear the bowl!*

training your puppy

Training your puppy is not easy but it is one of the most rewarding experiences you can share with a dog. As we have said before, dogs do not speak our language and do not learn as easily as people do, so you need a lot of time and patience to train a puppy.

When you are training your puppy, rewards are very important. If something a puppy does is rewarded — with a food treat, a toy, praise, or petting — it is likely to do it again. If the action doesn't get a response, the puppy might not repeat it. For example, if you are teaching your puppy to sit on command and you give a food reward each time he sits in front of you, the puppy will learn to sit when told, in the hope of getting another treat.

Puppies also do things that they find fun or self-rewarding. These natural actions include digging, barking,

Tasty treats are often the way to your puppy's heart! Used carefully, treats will help you train your pet.

chewing, chasing, and eating.

Puppies love to get attention, too. If a puppy does something bad, like stealing your toys, and you laugh at him, the dog may think stealing is a game and do it again!

dogs don't speak English!

If you have seen a Lassie movie or *102 Dalmatians*, it might be tempting to think that dogs understand every word that humans say! Although dogs can learn what individual words mean by remembering how they sound and what happened after they were spoken, our speech is like a foreign language to them. Instead, dogs watch our body language and the expressions on our faces.

learning the language

Training a dog is like learning to speak to a person from a foreign country. Person and dog need to learn a little of each other's language and use body language that both understand. Shouting, repeating the same words over and over, and becoming frustrated do not help. The clearer and calmer the words and gestures are, the more your puppy will understand.

your dog's dictionary

It is confusing for a puppy if you use the word "sit" but another member of your family uses the words "sit down" to mean the same thing.

dog dictionary

word	meaning
....	....
....	....
....	....
....	....
....	....

example dog dictionary

word	meaning
Puppy's name	Look at me
Sit!	Put your bottom on the floor
Down!	Lie on the floor
Come!	Come to me
Off!	Get off the furniture
Leave it!	Don't touch

It is useful to create a "dog dictionary" of all the words that you and your family are going to use in training. When you have agreed what each training word should be and what you mean by them, paste the list on the refrigerator door and make sure that everyone reads it. Look at the examples above.

Parental Guide

Punishment is neither necessary nor warranted. Children and adults should not smack, shake, or shout at dogs. Reward-based methods are fun, simple, and effective. If you have a problem with your puppy's training, ask your veterinarian to refer you to a training class.

Treats of varying deliciousness for rewards (or "reinforcers") when clicker training (see next page) kept handy in a pot.

clicker training

If you don't have a clicker, the same effect can be achieved by "clicking" with your tongue, or by using an "action" word.

Clicker training is one of the most modern ways of training. It is also fun for you and the puppy. Clicker training means that you do not have to push, pull, or otherwise force your puppy to do anything.

what is a clicker?

A clicker is a small plastic box with a tiny sheet of metal inside, like the one below. When you press the clicker's button, the sheet makes a loud "click, click" sound. Over a very short period of time, your puppy can learn that the click sound means food, toys,

or praise will be given for obeying a command — rewards for good behavior. The sound "marks" the behavior that earned the reward, like a teacher putting a checkmark next to a correct answer in a school book.

If you do not have a clicker, don't worry. You can still use clicker training, as long as you always use the same word or sound instead of the sound of a clicker. You can use a word, such as "yes" or "right," or even make a double-click sound with you tongue against the inside of your mouth.

timing skills

Using the clicker makes the timing of rewards easier for you and your puppy to understand. The clicker is used as soon as the dog does the right thing, so he knows what earned the

reward. It also means the dog can be creative and learn what triggers the "click" sound — and the reward — and what doesn't.

Dogs that are trained with a clicker can perform amazing feats. They can be trained to help disabled owners by switching lights on and off, operating elevator buttons, and even bringing in the newspaper!

To begin with, your puppy is sure to make mistakes. Nobody's perfect. Ignore mistakes — do not click or give a treat, and **never** shout at or punish the dog. Your puppy will soon work out that only the right responses earn rewards.

This 16-week-old Labrador pup has been trained to take a treat very gently from a child's hand.

below: *Clicker training does not always need food treats as rewards — you can do as well with a favorite toy.*

right: *Dogs may love their owners, but they still need rewards for good behavior!*

Parental Guide

Many dogs owners believe their pet should do what they tell him because he "loves" them. Dogs need a reward for their actions but they can learn that praise is also rewarding. While praise can be a powerful tool, most puppies need more than praise to motivate them. Find out what your puppy likes most — small pieces of tasty food or a favorite toy are usually best.

first lessons in training
1 attention and sit

Using a food treat as a lure is quick and easy.

Remember to be calm and patient with your puppy. Use the clicker or your chosen clicker word as soon as the dog does the right thing, then give a treat. Always use the same clicker sound and remember to only use the words in your dog dictionary (*see page 61*).

pay attention

Make sure you and your puppy are somewhere quiet, in your home or outside. Have some really tasty, small treats ready. If you have a clicker, hold it behind your back — there is no need to point it at the dog and never click too close to the puppy's ears.

1. Say your puppy's name in a clear, happy voice.
2. As soon as she looks at you, click or use your clicker sound.
3. Give a reward.
4. Repeat this three or four times.

Soon, your puppy will start to understand the meaning of the clicker sound and will react to it, thinking, "Great, where's my treat?!" You will also have taught the dog to pay attention when you say his or her name.

Practice this as often as you can to make it really perfect. Now you are already to move on to other lessons.

It's time to begin training your puppy! You first need to be able to get the dog's attention — if the puppy is ignoring you, you can't teach anything. When she is watching you, start with the simplest but most useful command — "sit"!

Training a puppy to sit for a treat.

sit on command

To teach your puppy to sit, you need a food treat to use as a lure — something that will get her attention. When the pup follows the command, the treat is given as a reward.

1. Keep quiet and show your puppy you have a treat in your hand. Put it on the dog's nose, right up close. Hold the food tightly so she doesn't take the food from your fingers.
2. Lift your hand up and back, so the puppy has to look up to follow your fingers. The movement of looking upward like this should make her bottom go down.
3. Your puppy is sitting! As soon as the dog's bottom hits the ground, click or use your clicker word, then give her the food treat.
4. Repeat this a few times. If your dog's front legs come off the ground, your hand is probably too high, so lower it a little next time.
5. Next say the word "sit" just before you lift the food treat. Use the clicker sound as soon as your puppy sits, then give the food. The puppy will begin to associate sitting with the word "sit." Congratulations!
6. Now you need to get your puppy to sit without using food. With no food in

your hand, ask her to sit. If the puppy obeys, click immediately, then give a food treat. If the pup does not sit when asked, use a hand movement to help — raise your hand over her head as before, but don't hold a treat. Give rewards for good efforts.
7. Practice until your puppy sits quickly every time. Give the sit command before the dog gets anything it likes — dinner, having the leash put on, being let out into the yard. Being obedient to the "sit" command is the dog's way of saying "please" and "thank you"!

Parental Guide

If your puppy is boisterous, you may need to guide your child's hand while he or she is using a food treat as a lure. This will give puppy and child more confidence.

using a food treat

Hold the treat tightly between your finger and thumb when luring your puppy with food. Give it to the dog by placing it on the palm of your hand or by dropping it on the floor.

Keep your puppy's attention with the food lure.

2 down and stay

lie down on command

"Down" needs a little more patience than "sit," because you have to wait for the puppy to do the right thing. Keep watching and be ready for the moment your dog lies flat on the ground.

below: *Lure your puppy into the "down" position with a tasty treat.*

1. Hold the food lure at the dog's nose, then slowly lower your hand down to the ground, directly between your pup's front paws. Hang onto the treat by turning your palm down, so the food is hidden under your hand. The dog will want to burrow his nose underneath your hand to get the treat.
2. You will be able to tell if the puppy is trying if he raises a paw to try and get the treat from your hand, the front end goes down in a bowing motion, or if the dog moves backward a little. All these things mean you just have to wait. Eventually the puppy's back end will drop to the ground, too.
3. The second your dog lies down, click or say your clicker word, then drop the treat to the ground and let the puppy eat it.
4. Repeat this several times, sometimes with food in your hand, sometimes without.
5. When the puppy will always lie down by following your hand to the ground, say the word "down" as you begin to lower your hand.

right: *Keep your puppy sitting by practicing regularly.*

"down" without a food lure

1. Now stand up straight. Show your puppy that you have a food treat, and then tuck your hand behind your back. Quietly ask your dog to "down," but don't help with a hand movement. Most dogs will try sitting, or even giving a paw, before having the idea that lying down might work. Be patient and try not to repeat the word "down."

2. The instant that your dog lies down, click or say your clicker word, then give a big reward — several tasty treats and a game!

3. Repeat this several times in several different places in the home and yard, until your puppy lies down on command anywhere and everywhere.

stay

Once your dog has learned to sit and lie down on command, you can teach him to stay in that position for longer, by waiting before you click and treat.

1. Ask your puppy to "sit" or lie "down," count to five, click or give your clicker word, then give a treat. If the dog gets up before you have finished counting, use the "sit" or "down" command and start counting again.

2. Ask the puppy to "sit" or "down," count to ten, click, then treat.

3. Ask the puppy to "sit" or "down," count to two, click, then treat.

4. Ask the puppy to "sit" or "down," count

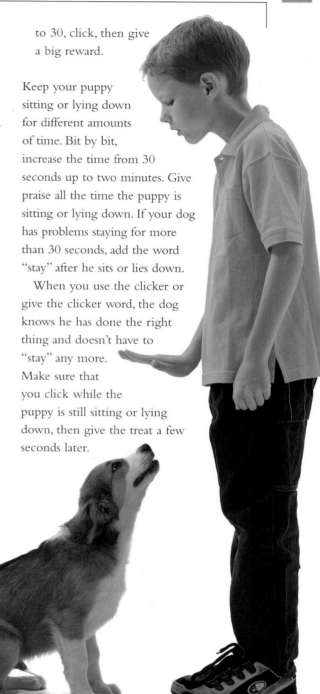

to 30, click, then give a big reward.

Keep your puppy sitting or lying down for different amounts of time. Bit by bit, increase the time from 30 seconds up to two minutes. Give praise all the time the puppy is sitting or lying down. If your dog has problems staying for more than 30 seconds, add the word "stay" after he sits or lies down.

When you use the clicker or give the clicker word, the dog knows he has done the right thing and doesn't have to "stay" any more. Make sure that you click while the puppy is still sitting or lying down, then give the treat a few seconds later.

3 returning when called

You should have already taught your puppy to pay attention (*see page 64*), so when you call the pet's name he looks at you. The next thing the dog should learn is to come to you when you call. This command is very useful. You can call your puppy into the home if you want him for something, for example, or call your dog away from trouble.

1. Stand in front of your puppy, say his name, and waggle the food lure in your hand. If the dog moves to you, click or give your clicker word, then give a treat.
2. Repeat this, but move backward a step or two. Encourage the puppy to come to you for clicks, praise, and treats.
3. Change the distance your puppy has to come to get the food — sometimes only one step, sometimes as many as 12 paces, and distances in between.
4. When the puppy comes to you every time you say his name, add the word "come" or "here" after the name.

You are now ready to add something. As soon as your puppy reaches you, touch the dog's collar, click or give your clicker word, and give a treat. This teaches the dog to come to you and then wait while you hold him or her before getting the reward.

If your dog is very slow or doesn't come when called, do not be angry — this will make the puppy less likely to come to you. Instead, show the puppy the reward you would have given, then put the food or toy

With your puppy at a distance, hold out a treat or toy as a lure, and say the puppy's name and "Come!"

away. Go back to the first lesson (*page 64*), and when your pet pays attention to his name, try teaching the "come" command again.

testing your puppy

Practice the "come" or "here" command by calling your pet for a click and treats, dinner, or a game when the puppy least expects it:

- Call your puppy to you from another room.
- Call your puppy out into the yard.
- Call your puppy inside from the yard.
- Call your puppy when you are sitting down.
- Call your puppy away from distractions.

As a reward for obeying the "Come!" command, let the puppy play with the toy.

Hansel and Gretel game

Some puppies need extra help before they will come to you when called, and the more fun you can make this, the better! In the fairy tale, Hansel and Gretel left a trail of bread so that they could follow it home — but birds ate it. In this version, you are going to leave a trail of food for your puppy to follow and eat!

1. Starting with the puppy by your side, walk a few steps away and drop a piece of food.

2. Encourage your puppy to find the food. As soon as he finds it, click and let the dog eat it.

3. Now move away a few more steps, call your puppy, and drop another piece.

4. Keep playing, moving further away, and soon your puppy will follow you around the home and yard like a little shadow!

Once your puppy comes when called, increase the distance he has to travel to enjoy his reward.

4 walking on the leash

Teaching your puppy to walk properly on a leash is difficult but very important. Walking with your dog in a park is fun and relaxing... but if the pup pulls on the leash, the trip is spoiled! Being pulled along by your pet is annoying and can be very tiring for you.

Dogs usually pull on the leash because they get rewarded for it. If they pull on the leash, they get to the park more quickly and can lead their owners to where they want to go. It should be the other way around, so as a dog owner you must learn to keep your pet under control.

Puppies need to learn when they are walking nicely on the leash, and this is where the clicker — or your clicker word — really helps. If your puppy pulls on the leash, stand still. Do not allow the dog to pull you for even one step! Do not take another step until the leash is loose. When the puppy is standing calmly and the leash is loose, let your pet know she has done the right thing by clicking and treating.

step by step

1. Put your puppy on the leash in the home or yard and stand still.
2. As soon as the puppy lets the leash go slack (loose) and looks at you, click and treat, then start walking in any direction you choose.
3. Watch your puppy carefully. If the leash is tight, stand still. Do not take a step until the leash is slack.

Teaching your puppy to sit quietly while having the leash put on is the first part of the exercise!

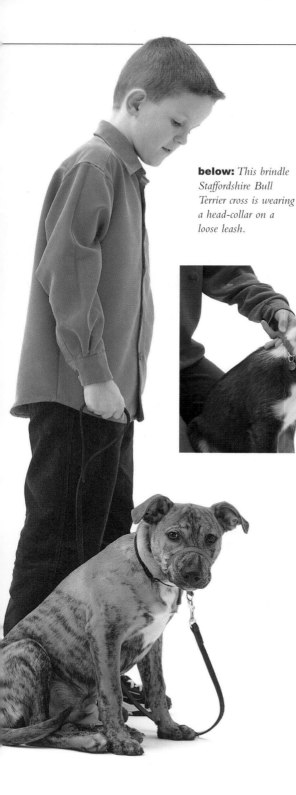

below: *This brindle Staffordshire Bull Terrier cross is wearing a head-collar on a loose leash.*

Parental Guide

If your puppy is a persistent puller, or if your children find the stop-start technique difficult, using a head-collar is a sensible idea. Head-collars allow you or a child to guide the dog more easily, so walking is much safer and more pleasant for the whole family. Click and treat when your dog is in the right place to hasten the training. All dogs can be taught to walk nicely on a leash and ordinary flat collar, or if necessary a head-collar. Choke chains, prong collars, and other so-called "correctional" devices are totally unnecessary and can easily cause injury, as can an improperly used head-collar.

left: *You should be able to put two fingers between the puppy's neck and the collar to ensure it is not too tight.*

4. Every time your puppy walks close by your side, so there is a loop of slack leash, click and treat.

5. Repeat this a few times, then stop and have a game.

6. Tuck food treat into a pocket. Click to the correct position — at your side, with the leash very loose — then produce the treat. Be generous with the food treats at first, then gradually reward only the best responses.

7. When you have practiced this in the home and yard, try walking the puppy in a park. Don't expect too much too soon. There will be a lot of sights and smells to sidetrack your puppy so at first you will stand still more than you walk forward. Be patient.

5 leaving objects alone

"Leave" or "off" is a very useful command if you don't want your puppy to steal your food! It tells your puppy not to touch things that you don't want him to have. There are many things you will want your puppy to leave alone, including human food, cats, clothes, litter in the street, and your toys.

Practice this part of your puppy's training for short periods of time but repeat regularly until the dog "leaves" a forbidden object every time you give the command. The more you practice, the better your puppy will get. Even the best trained dogs may not be able to resist food if left within their reach, so always make sure that you put food away if you are going to leave the puppy alone.

To teach your puppy to leave things, first

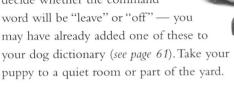

Even very young puppies can learn to "leave" things alone.

decide whether the command word will be "leave" or "off" — you may have already added one of these to your dog dictionary (*see page 61*). Take your puppy to a quiet room or part of the yard.

1. Hold a food treat in your hand and close your fingers around it. Rest your fist on your knee.
2. Wait while your puppy sniffs, licks, and nibbles at your fist, trying to get the food. Do not say anything and do not move your hand away.

Train your puppy to "Leave!" by holding the food tightly in your closed hand. Wait until your puppy takes his nose away before clicking and treating.

3. Watch carefully. As soon as your puppy turns his nose away from your hand, even for a second, click or use your clicker word, then give the treat. You will need to concentrate very carefully at first.

4. Repeat this several times.

5. Repeat the lesson, but this time wait until the puppy takes his nose away from your hand for two seconds, then click and treat.

6. Keep repeating the lesson, increasing the amount of time that your puppy's nose has to stay away from your hand to ten seconds.

   At this point you can add the word "leave" (or "off") in a calm voice, not a threatening one.

7. Next, repeat the exercise but say "leave" and show the food on your open hand. If the puppy tries to take it, close your fingers around the food — do not pull your hand away.

8. With regular practice, most puppies quickly learn that the word "leave" means that they must not touch. Eventually dogs learn that "leave" means that they should leave an object or animal alone, too.

Parental Guide

If the puppy tries to snatch food treats or is not gentle with its mouth during this exercise, you may have to start the teaching the "leave" or "off" command yourself. Once the puppy has started to move away from the hand holding the food, your child can take over the training.

tempting food

Start teaching the "leave" command using pieces of dry dog food. Later, use tastier food, such as pieces of chicken or liver. These are more tempting and so are harder for your puppy to resist.

Concentrate while you teach your puppy to wait for food.

6 retrieving objects

Some puppies naturally run out and pick up toys and objects that have been thrown and bring them back to their owners. But they may need encouragement to let go of the toy.

For other puppies, lots of rewards must be given before they will even hold an object. This exercise helps most puppies to hold things with confidence. Remember to practice — your dog won't learn if you only try to teach a lesson a few times.

1. Start with a toy or object that your puppy likes — a rag, cardboard tube, or a dog toy. Have some tasty treats ready.
2. Holding the object in your hand, offer it for the puppy to sniff. If your dog even touches it, click or use your clicker word, then give a treat. Repeat this a few times.

3. Next wait until the puppy tries to take the object in her mouth. Let the puppy hold it for one second, then click and treat.
4. Gradually increase the time the puppy holds the object to about 20 seconds, then click and treat. When the object is held for 20 seconds every time, add the word "hold" just before the dog takes the object.
5. Next put the object on your knee or on the ground, and ask the puppy to "hold."
6. When your puppy takes objects from your knee or the ground, your pet will understand that "hold" means "go, pick it up, and bring it back" for a click and treat.

Usually, playing with toys is rewarding for the puppy, so clicks and treats don't have to be used for long. Your dog will play retrieve games just for fun!

retrieval exercises

If your puppy is good at retrieving, encourage it to retrieve:

- A dog toy
- A cardboard tube
- A small, empty plastic bottle
- A glove
- An old metal spoon
- A bunch of keys

all the way

Some dogs learn that it is more fun to make their owners chase toys and balls than it is to fetch the objects themselves! Make sure that your puppy brings toys all the way back to you when you play retrieving games. If your dog drops the toy and then hovers over it, waiting for you to pick it up, encourage the puppy to hold the toy and deliver it into your hand.

retrieving metal

Metal objects — such as the spoon and keys listed for retrieval exercises — are usually more difficult for your puppy to hold. If your dog doesn't want to hold a metal object, use lots of encouragement and lots of practice.

pup-mail!

Once your puppy has learned to retrieve, you can play all kinds of games together. Fetching and carrying is very useful if you want to send messages to friends or family who may be in a different room, or out in the yard.

Write your message and roll it inside a cardboard tube to protect it from being chewed. Now ask your puppy to find the other person. The receiver may need to help at first, by calling the dog's name, but once your puppy has the idea, she will deliver your messages every time.

Encourage your puppy to sniff and follow a toy, then have a game with it. The big question is, will he bring it back?

how to behave around dogs

Usually, dogs are wonderfully friendly creatures, who like the people that they meet. But, even the friendliest puppy can be in a bad mood or seem a little grumpy. This might be because the puppy is feeling ill or is tired, but a dog cannot tell you what's wrong. Instead, the puppy may growl, show his teeth, or even snap at you. If this happens, it is very important that you listen to what the dog is telling you and back off, then immediately tell an adult.

when you are outside

It's sensible to remember that not all dogs you meet outside will be as friendly as the one you have at home. Some dogs do not like being touched by strangers, so it is important to always ask the owner if you may pet their dog before you do so.

meeting strange dogs

Occasionally, you may see a dog without his owner, perhaps in a park or on the street. Do not touch him. The dog could be frightened or feeling defensive, so keep away from him and tell an adult where you saw him.

If a dog that you don't know comes straight toward you while you are out, try to stand still and act like a tree! Do not look directly at the dog, because staring can seem like a threat. Try to keep quiet and wait for the dog to go away, then calmly walk off and tell an adult.

Never run, wave your arms around, or scream. All these actions can make the dog think that you are frightening, and he may think he needs to defend himself.

Some dogs will chase moving objects. The owner should stop this, of course, but if you are chased by a dog, do not shout or scream. Instead stop moving and stand still. Face the dog but don't look directly at him. This should give the dog the chance to calm down

If a dog chases you when you're on a bike, get off and place the bike between you and the dog. Keep quiet and keep still, then ask an adult for help.

and the owner a chance to come and put him back on a leash. If you are riding your bike and get chased by a dog, stop, and slowly get off. Keep the bicycle between you and the dog and wait quietly for the dog to lose interest and walk away.

Parental Guide ⚠️

Many children are bitten by dogs each year — but usually by their own pets rather than strange dogs. This is why socialization and training is so important.

If you have any concerns about your pet's behavior, do not wait, ask your veterinarian for a referral to a behavior specialist or trainer.

barking dogs

Never tease a dog that is barking at you from behind a fence or gate, like the one in the picture below. This is very unfair, and potentially dangerous. If you knock a ball over a fence or gate, do not climb over to get it. Ask an adult to get it for you. Some dogs are very friendly outside, but will defend their territory, such as the yard, and may become aggressive if you approach them.

below: *This pack of dogs is deciding whether an approaching stranger represents a threat to their territory. Once one barks, so will the others.*

understanding a dog's body language

Dogs do not speak as we do. And yet you can learn to understand what your puppy is "saying" by learning dogs' body language. Just like us, dogs use facial expressions and movements to show how they are feeling. Some expressions used by people are quite similar to those used by dogs, but other expressions mean completely different things.

unhappy messages

Dogs give each other warnings if they do not feel happy. If you see your puppy or any other dog show these expressions or movements, leave him or her alone:

Stops moving

This means that the dog is feeling unsure and wants to be left alone. Dogs often do this if they have a bone or other item that they want to guard. Never try to take the item.

Growling

This should be obvious. The dog is clearly saying "go away"! Or it may be playing.

Showing their teeth

Dogs warn us that they may bite by lifting up their lips and showing their teeth. This is like saying, "Look at my weapons!" However,

don't forget that all dogs show their teeth a little when they are panting or have their mouths open (as you can see in this picture on the right, below); this is not aggressive.

human expressions		dog expressions	
Expression	**Meaning**	**Expression**	**Meaning**
Smiling	Happy	Showing their teeth	Angry
Frowning	Annoyed	Wrinkling the brow	Concentrating
Eyes wide open	Surprised	Eyes wide open	Frightened
Eyes half closed	Sleepy	Eyes half closed	Friendly
Staring	Interested	Staring	Threatening

left: A play-bow is a clear invitation to play — no matter who the friend is!

right: With front end down and bottom in the air, this Border Collie puppy does a play-bow.

Play-bow

The dog puts his head low to the ground and his bottom and tail high in the air, as if he is going to pounce. This is an invitation to play.

Lifting a paw

Dogs often offer you a paw. This is like us shaking hands and shows that the dog is friendly.

Bounces

Some dogs, especially when they are puppies, bounce — their two front feet pounce on the ground. Puppies sometimes bounce then run away as an invitation to be chased!

tail positions and wags

A dog's tail tells you a lot about how he is feeling — if you can see it properly. Some breeds of dog have their tails docked or shortened, so it's difficult to use their tails to guess their mood.

Dogs that are happy and friendly show big, wide wags of the tail that say they are really

Hackles up

Dogs can raise the hair on the back of their necks to make themselves look bigger than they really are. This is often because he is frightened. It's best to leave a dog alone if his hackles are up, because frightened dogs sometimes bite.

Crouching and tucking the tail under

This dog is fearful and worried. A scared dog will probably run away if he can, but don't approach because he could bite.

friendly messages

At other times, dogs use body language that show how friendly they are. If you see dogs do any of these things, he probably wants to play:

Tail high and paws up, this puppy shows confidence and eagerness.

above: *With his tail tucked tightly between his legs, this puppy is showing anxiety.*

pleased to see you. But a wagging tail does not always show happiness.

- A tail held high and wagging vigorously shows confidence and even aggression.
- A tail held low, wagging gently, may show uncertainty.
- A tail tucked underneath the dog shows it is worried.

why does my dog yawn?

Dogs yawn for all the same reasons we do! They yawn because they are tired, bored, or because they saw another dog or a person yawning. Dogs also yawn to show that they are nervous or feel under pressure. If your puppy yawns during training, you may need to be more gentle with your pet.

Just plain worn out! With his tongue extended to its full length, this dog is about to yawn.

why does my dog lick?

Dogs lick people as a sign of affection. This action first starts when dogs are puppies and they are licked clean by their mother, which feels comfortable and reassuring. Puppies lick their mother to show that they want to be fed. By licking around her mouth they hope that she will regurgitate some food for them. This action is never forgotten, so some adult dogs lick their human owners to show affection.

does my dog have dreams?

Dogs seem to have dreams. They can often be seen wriggling their feet, wrinkling their noses, and growling while they are asleep! Some sleeping dogs move their feet and tail, as if they are running. However, humans will never know what dogs really dream about.

why does my dog have big teeth?

Dogs are omnivores, which means that they eat both meat and vegetables. Wild dogs have to hunt for their dinner — they chase, catch, and kill their prey. Their large front "canine" teeth are pointed and hooked like fangs, so they can grip the prey and tear the flesh. The back teeth are shaped for grinding up bones and muscle; human back teeth are used for chewing.

can my dog tell the time?

Your dog can't use a watch but does have a good idea of time. Many dogs are very clever and know when they should be fed or when their owners should be back from work or school. Some dogs become restless or sit by the front door when it's nearly time for a member of the family to get home. Other dogs wake their owners at the same time every morning — very useful unless it's a weekend!

does my dog recognize people?

Yes! Dogs have very good memories and can recognize people and other dogs, often by the way they smell. They can remember people they haven't seen for a long time or have only met a few times before. Dogs have been known to make their own way back home after getting lost, because they know the right direction to take.

So this is what teeth are for?! A Lakeland Terrier-Border Collie cross gnaws a juicy knuckle bone.

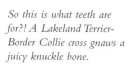

fun with your puppy
1 games to play indoors

Just because it's raining doesn't mean your puppy has to sleep all day! Dogs are always ready to play. Try some of these indoor games, and then think up some of your own. Your puppy will love it.

have a hunting party

Puppies can search for toys, food, or people indoors. Hide and Seek games are easy to play, either with humans or objects that your dog particularly likes.

Ask your pup to wait in one room, while you hide a toy or biscuit — or yourself — in another. Make the searches easy at first. Be encouraging and act really pleased when the puppy finds the item.

As your dog gets better at this game, you can make it more difficult by hiding a special item. For example, some dogs can be trained to search for the smell of a particular object, such as a coffee bean.

fun with food

Wild dogs have to hunt for their food. In our homes, dogs don't need to make any effort at all — their dinner arrives in a bowl in front of them!

To make food more interesting, encourage your puppy to work for it. If you give the dog dry food, scattering it around the home will keep the puppy busy searching for it. The dog's enthusiasm and tail-wagging will increase the better she gets at the game.

Dogs fed on wet food — meat and canned

Getting treats out of a plastic bottle is fun.

cheap and cheerful

Plastic water bottles can be fun toys. Remove the lid and push a dog biscuit inside. Your puppy will have to roll and shake the bottle to get the treat out!

fun with boxes

A large, safe cardboard box can provide hours of fun, while allowing your puppy to use up some destructive energy. Place the box upside down at first, with toys or a treat underneath, then upright with puppy treasures inside.

A "nest" of boxes is a clever idea — put one box inside another, and so on, with a treat sandwiched between them. Putting a large ball inside a box is another idea. Terriers in particular love putting their heads right in and "digging" balls out

food — can enjoy a version of this game. Split the food up into as many small pieces as you can and hide them in dishes around the house. Some dogs can be taught to retrieve each dish as they clear it of food. Be careful — eating wet food quickly and then rushing around can make a puppy sick, so only put a teaspoon of food in each dish.

Treats are more fun if they are hidden inside toys, bones, and even paper sacks. Stuffing food into a hollow Kong toy (*see page 50*) keeps dogs amused for hours. Most dogs find bouncy rubber Kong toys very exciting, and once stuffed with food such a toy is

almost irresistible.

Try putting different types of food inside a hollow toy to see whether if affects your puppy's interest or the time taken to empty it. Kongs can even be put into the freezer once packed with food, to create a frozen treat for dogs!

hunting and searching

Place a small piece of cheese or ham inside a cardboard tube (like the center of a roll of toilet paper). Fold the ends of the tube down to keep the treat inside. Show this to your puppy and let her sniff it.

Keep the puppy in one room, while you hide the tube in another room. Release your puppy to search for the tube and see how many seconds it takes the dog to find the tube. You can give encouragement but don't show the puppy where the tube is hidden.

score

5 seconds or less and brings tube	25 points
5 seconds or less	20 points
10 seconds or less	15 points
20 seconds or less	10 points
30 seconds or less	5 points
over 30 seconds	0 points

through the maze

Use your imagination to invent a "maze" for your puppy. A good way to make a maze is to get a large cardboard box or carton and open up the top. Carefully cut three sides of the bottom, to make a flap door, and lie it on its side. This makes a simple tunnel for your puppy to pass through.

A treat is hidden under the cup while the puppy watches.

At first the puppy just sniffs around the cup.

At first, hold the flap door up and place a toy or treat on the other side. When your puppy confidently walks through the tunnel every time you put something on the other side, drop the flap down. The dog will need to push through the flap to reach the prize. How long does it take your puppy to reach the toy or treat?

score

5 seconds or less	25 points
10 seconds or less	20 points
20 seconds or less	15 points
30 seconds or less	10 points
over 30 seconds, or goes around the box	0 points

treat under the cup

Put an old plastic cup or beaker upside down over a delicious food treat. Your puppy needs to work out how to get the treat, without any help from you! Count the seconds it takes her to reach the treat.

Some puppies move the cup with their feet, others nudge it away with their nose, or even pick it up by the handle. Any method is allowed, but you must not help your puppy get the treat.

score

5 seconds or less	20 points
10 seconds or less	15 points
20 seconds or less	10 points
30 seconds or less	5 points
over 30 seconds	0 points

In this similar game, a bone is hidden under a dog blanket instead of a cup.

The puppy can smell the treat hidden under the blanket and begins to "dig."

But then he begins to use his nose. He needs something to push the cup against, so it can be tipped over.

Once the cup is overturned, the treat is revealed and the puppy enjoys crunching into it!

A pair of knees are perfect to push the cup against!

learning through play

In the wild, dogs divide their time between sleeping, hunting, eating, and playing. Play keeps the pack together and maintains strong bonds between family members. It also allows each pack member's weaknesses to be found, then during a hunt one member can support another's weak side or take over the chase when a dog becomes tired.

genius or could do better?

Add the points from all three games together to get your puppy's overall learning score:

25 or more . . . . genius!
20 or more . . . . very bright
15 or more . . . . above average
10 or more . . . . needs more practice
5 or more . . . . a long way to go
less than 5 . . . . try again when your puppy is awake!

teenage wolves

All dogs, no matter what their age, like to play. It's thought that domestic dogs are "neotonized." This means that they never grow up to behave like real adult wolves — only like teenaged ones!

The digging works, and the puppy gets the treat!

2 games to play outdoors

on the right track

Teaching your dog to "track" — follow a scent trail — is fun and stimulating for you and your puppy. All dogs can track, as they have a built-in ability to follow smells on the ground and in the air.

To teach your puppy to track, you first need to lay a simple trail. Without your dog, go into the yard first thing in the morning to lay a trail. It's best to lay a trail on grass, as the puppy will be able to smell the crushed blades.

Walk in a straight line for ten steps and place something wonderful — food or a toy — on the ground. Turn around and walk back over the same footsteps that you have just taken. Leave the track for about ten minutes, then take your puppy out on a leash to find the starting point. Let the dog lead you to the reward and let him eat it, or give praise.

At first, many dogs look for the reward rather than sniff for it, so use your hand to encourage the puppy to look at the ground and use his nose. Once your puppy learns the rules of the game, gradually make the trails longer until the scent *has* to be followed

because the treat or toy is out of sight. Play, treat, and jump up and down like crazy when the dog tracks the trail to the target!

dog soccer

Teaching a dog to touch or push an object with its nose or foot can lead to lots of exciting games outside. Imagine playing real soccer with your puppy, without worrying that the ball will be burst!

1. Be ready with your clicker, or clicker word, and a food treat or toy.
2. Show your puppy the object, such as a soccer ball, holding it to the side of the dog's nose, about one inch away. Most dogs automatically reach forward to sniff an unusual object — click or say your clicker word and give a treat the instant the puppy

left: Since most dogs are curious enough to sniff at a strange object, it's not difficult to train your puppy to push a soccer ball with his nose.

sniffs the ball. If your dog doesn't do anything, tap the object and then click and treat the puppy for even glancing at it.

3. Repeat this process a few times. Most dogs soon make the connection between touching an object and the signal that they have done the right thing. Click and treat every time the puppy touches it.

4. Now hold the object a little further away (so the dog has to move), down under the chin (so the puppy has to bend its head downward), or slightly raised (to make the dog stretch).

5. Once your puppy has mastered touching the ball wherever it's held, place the object on the floor, or hold it up in the air for the dog to jump to reach.

You can also use a clicker and treats to encourage your puppy to use his feet to paw at a ball.

6. Next, wait for your puppy to push the ball a little harder, so it rolls along the ground, then click and treat. Practice until the dog pushes the ball to you, then you can push it back again. Always keep the ball out of sight when you are not training.

To teach a puppy to touch an object with its foot, give a reward for foot movements toward or on the object. Dogs vary in their ability to use their feet to touch things, but once they understand the concept of "touch" with their noses, most get the general idea very quickly.

round-robin recall game

For this game, you need one puppy or dog, some members of your family or friends, food treats, and dog toys.

1. Arrange all the people so that they are standing in a circle.
2. One person holds the puppy, then quickly names someone else in the circle.
3. The person who has been named calls the puppy and gives a treat or plays with a toy as soon as the puppy comes. Then they name someone else who must call the puppy.

sure the puppy always gets good rewards for coming. Perhaps the human winner of the game should get a reward, too!

square dancing

1. Place four markers in a square pattern in the yard, about six feet (2m) apart. With your puppy on the leash, walk up to the first marker and ask the dog to sit.
2. Next walk the dog quickly to the next marker and give the "down" command.
3. At the third marker the pup should sit again, and at the fourth one ask the dog to lie down again.

Have a friend time you from start to finish, using a stopwatch or a watch with a second hand, and see how quickly you can do this. Then let your friend have a turn and see if they can beat your time.

across the page: *Encourage your puppy to run after objects, pick them up, and bring them back to you.*

4. The puppy must go to the caller within 20 seconds, or that person is out of the game! When this happens, another person is named by the last successful player.
5. If all the people are very good at this game, give them only ten seconds to get the puppy to come to them each time. Make

To increase the challenge, add time penalties. For example, a five-second penalty is added to your time if you need to touch your puppy to get him to sit or lie down. Five seconds are also added to your time if you have to repeat the word "sit" or "down."

Remember, though, you and your friend must not get so excited about beating your time that the puppy gets accidentally abused or frightened.

above: *Those that play together, stay together. Spend time each day playing with your puppy.*

right: *She wants a walk! You can train your puppy to bring you the leash.*

fetch, fetch, fetch...

This game helps to teach your puppy to listen to you at a distance, and to retrieve objects.

1. Use chalk to draw a line across the yard, or place some markers to form a line.
2. Put at least eight dog toys or safe objects out beyond the line, in two rows of four objects.
3. Have your puppy sit behind the line. You should stand ten or 20 feet from the line.
4. You now have 30 seconds to get your puppy to fetch as many toys as possible! You are not allowed over the line, so use lots of encouragement and praise when your puppy shows interest in the toys and to encourage the dog to bring them to you.

below: *Retrieving a softball.*

3 sports to try

agility

Agility is an exciting sport for dogs and their owners. Dogs are taught to overcome various obstacles, such as jumping through tires, running through tunnels, and weaving in and out of a line of poles. Any breed can take part in agility contests, although Border Collies are among the fastest.

across the page:
Obedience training is important. Here a Yorkie cross breed puppy is given the hand signal for "stay" in the "down" position.

right, top to bottom:
A Golden Retriever going over a jump in an agility competition.

An owner gives her Yorkshire Terrier a clear "over" signal to take the jump.

Intrepid adventurer: a Jack Russell trots along a dog walk.

A Miniature Schnauzer on a mini seesaw.

As agility training involves jumping over hurdles, the dog's legs need to be strong — dogs younger than one year should not compete. Basic obedience is needed, because dogs are trained off-leash and are likely to come into close contact with people and other dogs — often at high speed (but not while in competition).

obedience

Obedience contests are popular around the world, as they show off the skills of both the trainer and the dog! They test heelwork, where the dog has to walk in a perfect position next to the owner's leg, stays — the dog has to sit, lie down, or stand in one position until told otherwise — and distance control, where the dog is guided by the owner's voice or hand signals.

Some obedience contests are run especially for children and their dogs. A good dog training class or club will help you prepare for these by teaching you the main exercises.

flyball

Flyball is great fun! Dogs usually run in teams, with one member at a time racing along a course. Each dog has to leap over several small hurdles, before reaching a box that contains a ball. The dogs are trained to step on a pedal on the box, which makes a ball come flying out. The dog runs back to the start line with the ball, then the next dog can go. The fastest team wins.

working trials

Working trials test a dog in several different areas: control work, tracking, finding hidden objects, and agility. This sport is ideal for those who love the outdoor life.

canine freestyle

Canine freestyle was originally based on obedience heelwork to music, but now includes tricks, such as the dog weaving in and out of the handler's legs, spinning on the spot, and walking backward — all in time to the beat of a song.

dog shows

Purebred dogs sometimes compete at conformation dog shows to judge how well they conform to the official "standard" appearance for their breed. In the show they are expected to stand still for the judge's examination and trot at the correct speed when asked to move. Many shows include junior showmanship classes especially for children, where children's handling skills are judged. Many dog clubs offer handling classes where you and your puppy can polish your skills.

Some small, fun shows have classes for crossbreeds and mongrels, as well as purebred dogs. You may be able to enter your puppy in a class titled "Dog with the waggiest tail" or "Most beautiful eyes"! A favorite class at many shows is "Dog that the judge would most like to take home"!

If you would like to try any of these sports, contact the Kennel Club for names and addresses of local dog trainers who will be able to help. It's a great way to meet new friends and have a fun day out!

4 trick training

give a paw

Many dogs teach themselves to give a paw —
or teach us to reward them for it! As
newborn puppies, dogs use their paws to press
on their mother's belly to get milk. Giving
a paw becomes a way of offering affection
and showing pleasure in later life.

*Puppies sometimes use a paw to pat a parent's muzzle
to ask for food or attention.*

1. First, encourage your puppy to sit in front
   of you. Give her a tiny piece of food from
   your hand.
2. Hold another treat tightly in your fist, close
   to the floor. Now watch carefully. The
   instant the puppy does anything with her
   paws, click or use your clicker word and
   release the treat.

3. Most dogs try to snuffle at the food with
   their nose or mouth. If you hang onto the
   food, your puppy will probably try
   touching your hand with a paw.
   Immediately click and treat when this
   happens. Repeat at least four times.
4. Now make a rule. Your puppy must make a
   deliberate move to touch your hand with a
   paw before getting the reward.
5. Now lift your hand a few inches from the
   ground. Your puppy will have to reach
   higher to touch you with a paw. Click and
   treat immediately for good attempts.
6. At the point where your puppy offers you a
   paw whenever you offer your hand, you
   can add the command word. Say "paw,"
   then wait. It won't be long before your
   puppy shakes hands on command.

high five!

Once your dog has got the idea of giving a
paw when you ask, move your hand away
slightly, so that the pup is "waving" in the air.
Click and treat. Your dog will soon offer you
higher and higher paw reaches — give me

left: *Hold the treat in your closed hand close to the floor. At first the puppy will just sniff at your hand.*

right: *Then, to get attention, he will dab your hand with a paw. Say "Paw!" and give the treat.*

below: *After a few sessions, your puppy should give a paw every time you say "Paw!"*

be a bear

This trick can be called lots of things: "be a bear," "be a penguin"… or simply "beg"! Your puppy will need a good sense of balance for this one, so be sure it is safe to try this first.

left: *This Golden Retriever sits up and pretends to "be a bear" while he holds a ball in his mouth.*

1. With your puppy sitting, hold a food treat a little way above the dog's head. If even one foot comes off the floor in an attempt to reach the food, click and treat.
2. Repeat this several times.
3. Now ask for more. Wait until both front feet leave the floor. Click and treat.
4. Gradually wait for the puppy to stand higher each time you practice. Give the dog time to balance and reach higher than before.
5. Finally, add a word that tells the puppy when to perform the trick — "bear" or "beg."

roll-over

Teaching your puppy to roll over on command makes grooming easy and means that your puppy is confident with you.

1. Encourage your puppy to lie down, using a food treat if necessary.

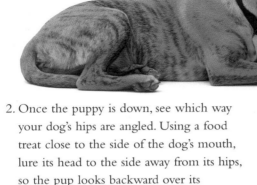

2. Once the puppy is down, see which way your dog's hips are angled. Using a food treat close to the side of the dog's mouth, lure its head to the side away from its hips, so the pup looks backward over its shoulder.

3. Keep the food treat close to side of the mouth and continue to lure the puppy over.

4. Encourage your puppy all the time. Keep a tight hold of the food treat while the dog rolls right over onto its back. Click and treat as soon as the pup rolls right over

5. Stop using food to lure your puppy over as soon as possible. Let the dog work out what gets the click and reward.

6. Add the words "roll over" only when the puppy performs reliably, without the use of a food lure.

7. Practice until your puppy can dive into a roll over from a standing position, then stand back up again. This looks really impressive!

Some breeds, such as Dobermans, find it difficult to perform this trick on hard surfaces, probably because they have bony, unprotected backs. Try practicing on a soft rug or duvet and click and treat for even the smallest effort in the correct direction.

take a bow

Once your puppy is able to perform all these marvelous tricks, she should be able to take a bow. Dogs bow to each other naturally as an invitation to play, so this isn't difficult to teach.

1. Hold a food treat on your puppy's nose and lower it slowly down between the front legs.

2. The puppy will follow the treat and her head will dip down, leaving the dog's bottom in the air. Click or say your clicker word and give the treat as soon as this happens.

3. If your puppy's bottom drops to the

left to right: *Encourage your puppy into a "down" position with a treat at his nose. Then (second picture) encourage him to roll over by following the treat in your hand. With practice* **above***, your puppy will roll over when he hears the command word.*

ground, gently use your hand under the belly to keep her rear in the air for a few seconds before clicking and treating.

4. When the dog finds this easy, say "take a bow" just before luring your puppy down. With enough practice you will find that you can train your dog to bow using just the words or a simple hand movement.

below: *A Border Collie play-bows with a toy.*

conclusion

All puppies are cute, cuddly, and adorable in the first few weeks. How your puppy grows up will be a reflection on how you — and your family — have cared and attended to its needs. Learning how your puppy thinks, communicates, and learns is very rewarding — and takes a lot of time!

From reading this book you will have learned that owning a dog is not the effort of a few moments, or even a few days. It's a job of caring for life. With the correct house training and obedience, the puppy becomes a member of the family — although with his or her own rules — and as an older dog will reward you with love and companionship.

You might care to join a local puppy socialization class so that both of you can receive professional instruction. But whether you do or whether you prefer to do your training only at home, enjoy your puppy training and — have fun with your puppy!

Muppet is an
English Springer Spaniel.
Say goodbye, Muppet!